Pagan Portals

Intuitive Magic Practice

A guide to creating a magical
practice using intuition

Pagan Portals
Intuitive Magic Practice

A guide to creating a magical
practice using intuition

Natalia Clarke

**MOON
BOOKS**

Winchester, UK
Washington, USA

JOHN HUNT PUBLISHING

First published by Moon Books, 2021
Moon Books is an imprint of John Hunt Publishing Ltd., No. 3 East Street, Alresford
Hampshire SO24 9EE, UK
office@jhpbooks.net
www.johnhuntpublishing.com
www.moon-books.net

For distributor details and how to order please visit the 'Ordering' section on our website.

ISBN: 978 1 78904 615 1
978 1 78904 616 8 (ebook)
Library of Congress Control Number: 2020936355

A CIP catalogue record for this book is available from the British Library.

Design: Stuart Davies

UK: Printed and bound by CPI Group (UK) Ltd, Croydon, CR0 4YY
Printed in North America by CPI GPS partners

We operate a distinctive and ethical publishing philosophy in
all areas of our business, from our global network of authors to
production and worldwide distribution.

Contents

Foreword   1

Introduction   3

Chapter 1: Intuition and Psychology   8

Chapter 2: Intuition and Dreams   15

Chapter 3: Intuition and Working with others   26

Chapter 4: Intuition and Journaling   29

Chapter 5: Intuition and Sacred space   33

Chapter 6: Intuition and Breathing   35

Chapter 7: Intuition and Creative Imagination   37

Chapter 8: Intuition, Trust and Ethics   39

Chapter 9: Intuition and Moon Cycles   44

Chapter 10: Intuition and Grounding   50

Chapter 11: Selecting Tools Intuitively   56

Chapter 12: Intuition and Candle Magic   61

Chapter 13: Working Intuitively with Spells   68

Chapter 14: Intuition and Working in Nature   72

Chapter 15: Intuition, Divine Feminine and Sacred
    Self-care   80

Chapter 16: Intuition and The Triple Goddess Aspects   95

Chapter 17: Casting Spells with Intuitive Drawings   100

Chapter 18: Intuitive Writing as a Spiritual Practice   104

Conclusion   108

Bibliograophy and Further Reading   110

About the Author   111

Foreword

Reading Natalia Clarke's work on Intuitive Magic Practice had a very powerful impact on me and led me to think deeply about the role intuition could play in my life. We tend to associate intuition with femininity, but at the same time, that intuition is something many women don't access. That it is seen as feminine in the first place can make it difficult territory for men to enter.

What we call intuition is often a very rational sort of process. Our bodies absorb far more information than our conscious brains can hope to process. Our thinking is far more distributed through our bodies than had previously been thought. So what comes back as a 'gut feeling' isn't something insubstantial or irrelevant. It can in fact be our best and most useful thinking, if we can access it and trust it.

If you have bought this book, the odds are you want your intuition back. When did you lose it? Who undermined it, or silenced it for you? What were you told? Because the loss of intuition is also the loss of self and self-trust. It's what happens when we don't have the self-confidence to hear our own voices, trust our own judgements and take our own discomfort or desire seriously.

Natalia offers us a healing journey. In building an intuitive magical practice, you can re-discover and reclaim parts of yourself. It's a process of taking back everything you were told you couldn't have and couldn't be, which makes it a glorious, subversive kind of witchcraft.

This book acted as a spell to change me, and I hope it will take you on a similar journey.

Nimue Brown

"The intuitive mind is a sacred gift and the rational mind is a faithful servant. We have created a society that honours the servant and has forgotten the gift."
Albert Einstein

Introduction

- Would you like to tap into your own sacred intuitive knowledge of the soul?
- Would you like to live your life in a magical, unique and meaningful way?
- Would you like to reclaim your voice that has been silenced or lost?
- Do you feel you have a lot of choices and directions, but not everything resonates?
- Would you like to create your own way of doing magic and feel empowered by it?
- Do you love and connect with nature and feel guided by the Elements?

In this book I hope you will find the right tools, techniques and, most importantly, inspiration that you can implement into your own intuitive spiritual magic practice. When reading these pages you will enjoy space and time to contemplate and explore your unique qualities and passions and experiment with trying new things to see what resonates through intuitive awareness and practice. I hope it will allow you to tap into what resonates with you intuitively and give you an entry point into a journey of discovering yourself and creating a practice built on your intuitive knowing; your own unique way of doing magic. You are the master of your own spiritual path. It is a joyous process to begin gathering things together into a magical practice that comes from inside of you. Not from a certain established tradition or a book, but from your own knowing, your own intuitive guidance system.

My perspective on the world is that nothing is static and there is always potential for change, growth and for moving forward. There is a constant evolution that happens every day, every week, every month, and we can all decide to take charge of our purpose. I am an experienced psychotherapist and an intuitive consultant working a lot with relationships, purpose and meaning, life and identity crisis, transformation through darkness and healing past experiences and trauma. As an intuitive practitioner I incorporate my knowledge and beliefs from the field of transpersonal psychology and mystic studies and use my natural-born gifts. I believe that your inner voice and your emotions are the two best navigating systems that you can use to guide you through life situations. My mission statement is *'Remember Who You Are'*. I have been living my life completely intuitively in every area and it has been my guiding star and something that anchors me in my experiences and self-knowledge. Connecting to your intuition and working with it creatively and authentically is a magical experience.

This book can also serve as a healing tool for those, who feel their souls have been wounded over their life time and they find themselves lost. It can provide empowering energy for those, who might have lost their voice and firm personal footing in life hiding behind un-serving masks and self-defeating actions. Intuition is the deepest voice within us, wise and reassuring that, when listened to, has our best interest at heart, never failing to direct us towards deep inner work.

I might say that this book is primarily directed at women, who have struggled with personal value, identity, and confidence, due to abusive relationships, betrayals, or family systems that have spanned generations. Having said that men can relate to some themes in this book through seeing the necessity in reawakening their unique voices from within. It is written for a female audience, yet some practices might appeal to a wider audience. Those told "boys don't cry" - swallowed their emotions and shut their hearts down, but also anyone, who has felt devalued in their bodies, their preferences of being in the world or ways of expression. It is in the crying that we truly feel ourselves and let our soul express our true feelings.

In this introduction to creating your magic practice using intuition, I encourage people to follow their own inner voice and tune into their own inner knowing and personal power. I give ideas on how to create spells and communicate with nature intuitively. Nature is always at the centre of my practice. I also offer examples from my personal practice in the form of journal entries that I have recorded over the years when working in nature and creating spells and rituals. I believe that we all have our own connection with the source energy and we all have an individual path to follow and missions to fulfil here on Earth. I always say "take what resonates with you and leave the rest". The material produced in this book is in the name of sharing my experiences when I first started my practice, and also sharing ways of creating, nurturing and maintaining your magical practice. Some prefer working purely intuitively, others feel better within a ritualistic practice of magic and many include both.

I started out many years ago on the path of nature-based spirituality and through a long journey of learning and experimenting I have discovered the best way for me to work and that is using my intuition in everything I do in my practice. I have been living a fully intuitive life ever since I rediscovered my spirituality. I use intuition in decision making, writing, drawings, music, creating spells, rituals and invocations, and in my communication with the Elements, places, and animals. The journey began for me when I first connected to a part of myself that had been asleep for a long time. I suspect many of my readers might relate to that, and there is something about the times we live in that makes this feel important; to re-awaken, to re-wild, and reclaim what has always been truly ours, sleeping within. I experienced this awakening within myself when someone on the outside (notice the intuitive inkling present in someone else) pointed out some qualities and abilities they sensed in me that I had no name for. I remember talking in a certain way and describing events and rituals that I would like to have done to deal with a particular issue, e.g. releasing some painful emotions or saying good bye to a loved one. The person listening saw the nature-based spirit, which I had bubbling up inside me, yet which I couldn't put a label or a description on. Following that experience I was gifted a Book of Shadows, an Athame (a double-edged ritual knife with a handle used in modern witchcraft) and a deck of Tarot cards. While exploring the meaning of all this information and familiarising myself with the objects gifted to me, I came back to my own deep alignment to the path of witchcraft. It took time making sense of my experience at first and until I tuned into myself and began relying on how I was feeling internally, none of it made sense other than on a concrete level of having information about things to do and how to do them. I put things away for some time and returned to it again later on and that time it felt like coming home; calm, peaceful and deeply knowing. Things began to open up for me, transform and manifest fast. Why then, you ask? I believe spending time with myself, by myself and taking myself off into nature on a regular basis, reading up on the subject of nature spirituality and all its aspects, building up a habit of visiting trees and listening to the wind, put me in touch with a part of myself that was hungry for more and ready to be used, asking to be brought back.

If you are on a spiritual path and, perhaps, finding it challenging to pinpoint what your path is, I suggest you relax. Remain open, patient and take it as a life-long commitment to finding your way while connecting to parts or aspects of whatever spiritual paths come your way or you become aware of while you are searching, researching and experimenting. Invite information and experience in and allow your intuition to transmit it to you and direct you towards what makes your soul sing. Is it a meditation part of a particular practice; working with herbs; are you attracted to candles and the element of fire is your primary source energy manifestation; working with spells with the moon cycles or are you more attracted to the sun; do you feel most comfortable with trees when working spiritually? Whatever practice surfaces for you, remember that things most likely will evolve and change over time, as your energy and life experience changes and as you get more confident in using yourself as the main tool for your practice. Intuition will be your best guiding tool while you are searching and especially as you are starting out. You are not lost, you are collecting parts of yourself that might have been hidden and resurrecting your own experience of spirit the way it has always been within you.

Chapter 1

Intuition and Psychology

Rational mind takes pride of place in our society. It has been this way for centuries. Intuition, however, has been treated as an unexplained phenomenon throughout history, yet it has always lived in all of us and yes, I refer to it as a living, breathing, moving and flowing phenomenon and, although invisible, we know it is there. Like any personality trait or a quality we were born with or a skill that we have, affinity for intuition can be developed and made a permanent feature in our lives, and lead to a whole new way of life. If we do not engage, it is like cutting off a part of ourselves that might not bother us; but that we will certainly encounter frequently in life, however our programming will tell us to ignore it. Intuition can be an invaluable addition, if not a central part of any spiritual practice; in fact, that is where it really fits as we learn to communicate with the outside world from within. As humans, we tend to consider ourselves as a leading force in everything we undertake rather than simply responding to what's presented to us in the external world. People, places, nature, towns, trees, rivers and objects can all call for an intuitive response. It is way of communicating, which is self-trusting and self-knowing. Through practicing this way you will get to know yourself on a level that deserves full recognition. It is linked with self-value and self-acknowledgement; viewing yourself as a spiritual and energetic being rather than just a physical body. In essence, intuition is your inner voice; that feeling, sense, or knowing that comes from you and *what if you listened to it?* That's where practise comes in and there are many ways to begin the process, which can then be applied to any area of your life and connect you spiritually to the world and work that you do. You might either apply it to a practice you have in place already or a new path that calls you. Intuition and imagination; the two are interlinked and intuition enhances imagination or accompanies it. You can tap into your creativity when led by intuition. It can be found in many arts, like writing, painting, singing or performing (ritual is partly performing), as well as, magic. Yes, it is a form of art too.

The thing with intuitive knowing is that it doesn't go away and can continue visiting you persistently in various ways to display the same message over and over until you notice and act. My question is why wouldn't you? What would happen if you didn't? It is a voice of your inner creativity and self-progression and what is a spiritual practice if not following a calling from within, often expressed through creativity and things you always wanted to do, but didn't think were important or of any value, or, perhaps, you thought that they wouldn't be acknowledged or that you will be laughed at and thought of as impulsive, naïve, or crazy. What if you did all those things and followed from within, would you not be happier? It is the same with a spiritual path that ultimately should lead to a more peaceful, satisfying experience for yourself and those around you. In many ways by not engaging with intuition, as a creative, living force within you are limiting your self-progression. One might suggest that it is the mind that pulls us forward on a journey of self-development and growth, but mind is devoid of feeling and sensations; it has to explain and make things logical, it has to abide by rules acceptable in the world. Intuition is made up of feelings, sensations in the body and experiences that cannot be explained, yet are real. Intuition is a function of your psyche that makes you whole and complete, but is underestimated frequently. Spirituality is a way of being rather than thinking and magic, ritual, sacred objects and divine energy cannot be accessed through the mind. We need intuition, feelings and sensations, which can communicate to us what we are experiencing and how it leaves us feeling. We must allow for something other than our mind to come into practice if we are to have the full experience.

Intuition is not to be understood. It is to be experienced. It is like a muscle that needs training and a skill that needs practice. It is like learning a foreign language. It is always there and speaking to us and it is a matter of whether we listen or not. Learning to stop and listen takes practice. It requires you going out of your comfort zone and into unfamiliar territories with trust. Practice with small things like "what to eat for lunch" or "what to wear to the office", etc. It requires you to follow what feels right, not what makes sense. Distinguish between imagination and various inner voices you carry inside through life-long conditioning and experiencing. What does your SOUL say? Often the three senses I present below (A gut feeling, Intuition and a Soul call) are used interchangeably, but are they the same? I would like to break it down here and believe there are some marked differences between the three, which you might find useful in your understanding of the intuitive function.

A 'gut' feeling

It is a feeling that something is either right or wrong. There is a sort of "tug" in your solar plexus area, hence the name – "a gut feeling". I believe a gut feeling often presents with a tinge of doubt, "not quite sure" signature to it. A feeling of "it might, it could be". It presents options, so to speak, therefore requiring a degree of discernment and a choice on your behalf. Because it is uncertain in its nature it is easy to ignore when it comes, as the mind often overrides it due to an element of hesitation. A gut feeling often comes as a forewarning of some sort, an anxiety provoking reaction. I'd say never ignore a "no" in your gut as it is led by fear, the positive function of which is to keep you safe. Fear here is not the enemy, but a protector. It wants to look after you. When it comes as a "yes", stay with it for a bit, do not jump into the vibration impulsively, as if acted upon too quickly it can turn benefits into a not so desired outcome. A gut feeling is different to intuition.

Intuition

This is of a sensation of deep knowing, often linked to divine inspiration like a flash, clear as a picture. You might experience an image, colour, direction, or a message. "Yes, I know and recognise it". That thing that writers often refer to as a muse or that thing that grabs them and keeps them in a flow. It is alive and has a very clear intention. Intuition is definitive, only one thing. It is fixed in the moment.

Another side of intuition is a personal story revelation, a piece of your own destiny, if you will, like a part of a series that is exactly right for you to see at a given moment. Intuition assists us in knowing ourselves better. It is usually very timely and aligned with what you are asking for, needing or doing. It is directly linked to Source/universe. This is the aspect this book is based on.

Soul Call

A soul call usually produces strong, overwhelming reactions in a person. It is linked to emotions like love, grief, sorrow or burning rage, something quite powerful, almost beyond ourselves, but very much part of us. The following reactions are examples: heart jumping out of your chest; breathing slows down or intensifies; can feel like something is dying in you (in a good way); you want to run for that thing that calls you (intense yearning).

Soul calling is very impulse-driven, animalistic and instinctual in nature hence very much an embodied sensation. It is an "I can't live without" type of feeling, an urgency to be more, to feel more, to jump out of the ordinary and join something beyond yourself that will lead you to your true self. Again very different from intuition.

Intuitive magic vs ritual magic

There are many ways of practicing magic and many spiritual paths to follow, or you can even create your own unique way of doing things and I encourage and invite you to create your own practice. It is so much more meaningful and deeply relational if you base your practice on your preferences and what resonates rather than following a prescribed set of rules and rituals. I base my practice solely on intuition (intuitive magic) and this relates to rituals I perform and spells I create. I align with the energy of the Source, nature, Gaia, The Goddess, or whatever divine entity I am drawn to, if any at all, and follow sensations in the body, symbols and images that come up for me and choose tools to work with as I go along. I usually either see, hear or sense energies. The way I would describe it is that information gets downloaded for me and I simply follow that information in creating a specific ritual or a spell.

This way there is a natural flow, no force, no attachment to an outcome, no artificial influences of any kind and it always works. One might say I flow with the intuitive energy if and when it comes in. If I am not called or specific energies are not present, I do not do anything. I do resonate with many elements of ritual magic, of course, and I use some techniques, such as, working with the Elements, for example, but I don't necessarily apply it in the prescribed order or following a particular rule or using particular phrases and words in invocations. I pick and choose and create my own magical musings always turning to my intuition first.

In my sharing of experience I encourage people to follow their own intuition and in this book I give ideas on how to do that; how to create spells intuitively and how to communicate with nature intuitively. There are no prescribed rules or ritual steps to follow. As I said in the Introduction, I believe that we all have an individual path to follow and missions to fulfil here, so our ways are going to be different. Take what resonates with you and leave the rest. All materials I produce are in the name of sharing experiences and ways of doing certain things and it might resonate with you or it might not. Some prefer working purely intuitively, others feel better with a ritualistic practice of magic, and others include elements of both. If you are wholly new to this, you may want more ritualistic and traditional to start with and then move into something more intuitive, or you may just dive in with intuition straight away. There is a beauty and richness in the diversity of paths available, and the important thing is that you pick one that resonates with you.

Intuitive guidance ignored is self-abandonment

We hear about self-love more and more these days in a sense that one must give oneself love in order to be able to give it out into the world. There is a strong dissonance of energy between giving and receiving in the world generally. Often we are good at giving, but terrible at receiving. Sounds familiar? We have bought into the idea of unquestionable self-sacrifice and understand receiving as bad, selfish, 'not allowed' and even shameful. What we do is simply abandon ourselves each and every time tricking ourselves into believing we are doing something right. We abandon our own internal system of guidance, which, if only we listened, would move us towards our highest self and our soul's purpose. We listen to one internal voice, which stems from years of internalised belief that we are bad if we don't give fully and we are not good enough if we allow ourselves to receive. By listening to one voice, we ignore another, which is our intuitive guidance from the soul carrying messages of love and compassion. We rationalise why something makes us feel good rather than accepting it. If something comes from the inside, then no, we don't have time to stop and listen, we must go on with doing and giving and often making ourselves invisible and ill in the process.

This cruel conditioning seems to be ruling so much of our

existence and robbing us of health, validation, recognition and sanity. Why is that? We are all part of one whole, part of the Source energy, which is unconditional love. YOU are divine and YOU are love, so fill your cup up and stop emptying it so readily under the illusion that you must do that. Learn to receive in equal measures to giving and rock that sacred feminine and masculine like we were meant to. Sounds tough? It seems to be the hardest task for almost all to re-learn self-love, to understand that we cannot separate from the whole. It is all one and we are built from the same material.

Our soul's purpose is abandoned through us abandoning our voice of love, our voice of intuition and we become unwell physically, emotionally and spiritually. This is because we often look for love, acknowledgement, and validation in the wrong place. We look outwards and not inwards. Looking inwards is something we need to re-learn; something we are to get acquainted with all over again; something we once knew well when we were born, but through human experience we forgot. When in times of despair our soul's song is not heard, we feel alone and we feel that we might as well not exist.

The Divine knows you and building a relationship with it and having a conscious link with your intuitive guidance system is a sure road back to yourself, to the natural state of being as one with it all. Breaking away from chains of our conditioning is tough and in breaking away we break down, but it is in breaking down we find a way towards the light.

Exercises

- Spend some time tuning into your intuition.
- Is it easy or hard for you to tell the difference between a soul call and an intuitive message?

Chapter 2

Intuition and Dreams

Psychologists explain intuition as material that comes from our unconscious and hence often dreams contain symbols and experiences that are not clear or can easily be explained, but the mystery of dreamlife is exciting and full of possibilities. Dreams create a certain energy, a feeling in us when we try to go over their content on waking and that's what we can use as a springboards in our spiritual practice. For example, a "Masculine energy" dream might ask us to work with that energy and ask us to explore questions like "what can you use in conscious life and your practice to work with the energy of the Sun"? Perhaps, doing fire spells (Fire is often associated with the masculine energy) to release and manifest what might be needed in life at that point. Dreams are a powerful form of intuition because they by-pass the ego and the linear mind to offer clear intuitive information. They bring guidance about healing, spirituality and overcoming difficult emotions (sometimes through the healing power of nightmares), telling you how to help yourself and others. They are complex in imagery and symbols and should be tapped into through the function of feeling rather than engaging the mind in dreams interpretation. You must find the resonance with dreams' elements through how they make you feel and from their insights will follow.

Pay attention to the following when working with dreams: colours, figures, images, animals, textures, light, relationships, dynamics, landscapes and most of all feelings your dream experience evoked in you. Free-associate with whatever you remember on waking, e.g. when you think of a number ten what comes to mind? What does a tall building mean to you? Follow your intuition and how you feel all the way through working with your dreams and see if you can discover certain resonance, a message, a release of a feeling, an answer to a question or any other insight.

Examples of dreams/intuition and how to work with them in your spiritual practice

The following examples are taken from my journal, and I have chosen them to illustrate ways of working with dreams to you:

"I was rushing around in a busy atmosphere filled with noise and people. I was aware of classrooms and a variety of textbooks, papers and materials everywhere. I had a strong feeling I didn't belong. I tried to join this group and that group and get involved with this class and that desperately trying to catch up. Catch up with what? I stopped and looked around and felt panic enveloping my body and mind. I must go on, I kept saying to myself, or I will be left behind. There was a studious atmosphere around the place and there were people of all ages and abilities present. Where do I fit? I carried on for a long time getting stuck in with various tasks and sitting down with books, plans and schedules until I stopped. I really stopped and realised I didn't have to do any of it. I had an education and already held several degrees and had been established for many years. What was it I was chasing? The voice inside repeated over and over, "You have to do what others do, you have to join in with the crowd." The truth was I didn't have to do any of it.

A feeling of immense freedom came over me and I felt relaxed and peaceful as I walked away from the idea of institutionalised society, as 'good' and 'right'; leaving behind conditioning and the rat race. What a feeling to know at any given moment that we can stop and say 'I don't actually have to, I am free as I am, any time anywhere and there are choices all around me.' A path of space and freedom opened up and I walked towards a beautiful sunrise."

I felt grateful, humble and free.

Authenticity dream

"I was given a bottle of silver and gold liquid that was meant to be put on my face like make-up. It felt luxurious on the skin and looked beautiful. I put it on all over my face and walked into a room with a long table where there were people sitting either side.

One side of the table loved it and admired my beauty. The other side preferred me without it.

There was a dilemma for myself. What did I like? What did I want to do? 'The mask' continued to feel wonderful on my face and looked truly stunning. It gave me a certain advantage and an edge. I felt that.

In the next scene I was heading towards some showers to wash my hair and there was a man, who said that if I washed my face off I would no longer be the most beautiful woman in the whole world and would become the second in line after some other woman. The man smirked and had an expression of warning about him as if to say, 'really think about what you want to do, think twice.' There was another man in the room, who had light hair and appeared very calm with a soft face; a complete opposite to the first man. Looking at him I knew instantly he didn't care much for my 'mask' or the way I looked at all. He saw deeper.

I decided to get rid of my face make-up and leave my hair unwashed and instantly felt lighter and more grounded. A very different feeling from when I felt I had an edge. Much softer.

I took the hand of the blonde man and we walked outside to the light. He appeared to have something lodged in the inner corner of his left eye. A thin stick or a string of some sort. I said to him that I would attempt to pull it out, but it might hurt. This felt like it had something to do with the way he was seeing things and, perhaps, the object lodged in there obscured his true vision. I started pulling the string out. It was very long. The man didn't flinch or change in any way, he just smiled gently at me.

We embraced and fell on the ground when I realised I had a pure white coat on and was lying in mud. For a second I was concerned, but quickly relaxed and, while in his arms no longer cared whether my coat *was ruined. His support and acceptance was all I needed."*

One of the best dreams I have ever had.

Spring Equinox dream

"I had an Ostara dream of giving birth, first to a girl and then a boy. They were two separate pregnancies and births and both spoke of healing, balance and transformation. As I began to wake up a sense of wonder, peace, joy and satisfaction laid over me with vivid presence. I was content.

Both births happened fairly quickly and naturally. They flowed the way, I felt, it was meant to be. A very physical experience yet easy, calm and trusting. It brought a true healing to my experience of childbirth in real life, which had been very traumatic. For many years my mind had blocked it out and forgotten it with my body carrying the trauma locked inside. I had birth dreams before, but nothing like this one. Last night it spoke of the way things get birthed into being and how when trust and knowing are present it can be a natural and easy process. We hear about it often yet it is not always so.

With Spring Equinox coming into life the importance of balance comes into place. Feminine and Masculine energies begin to birth into what is to become a union later on in May. It felt magical and so timely to birth that experience of both as equal into the world. Both the girl and the boy were born safely and into a lot of love around them."

Birth dreams often refer to a new beginning, a journey of growth and potential transformation. Spring is a vulnerable and delicate time of transition. Many things get born into the world during spring, but not everything survives. It can be a time of doubt and trepidation, but also hope and a possibility.

For a few nights prior to my Ostara dream I dreamt of dead bodies, body parts and holding on to stuff that had died some time ago. Those dreams are frequent and come about when it is time I let go of the weight of the past and allow some parts of myself to die and bury it not in shallow graves, like it is often in my dreams, but deep within the darkness and nourishment of the earth. Death dreams are always followed by birth dreams.

This particular Ostara dream also told me that a birth doesn't have to be painful, traumatic, rushed or unsupported. It can be truly invigorating and rewarding work and the results are delicate and hopeful like nothing else.

A heart in a cage dream

"My intentions for this year are to attempt the process of releasing pain that has taken residence within my energetic bodies for a very long time. I have carried it all with devotion and protection. No one could ever be allowed to come in.

Expansion into love, beauty, softness and courage is a path I would like to step on this year. Here comes a challenge of not doing everything by myself, not suffering in silence and allowing someone else to show me love and help me heal.

Last year I managed to learn and embrace the concept of not allowing MORE pain to come in through saying 'no' and standing much stronger in my power. It has been very hard, but did pay off in huge ways and I have been able to see and feel the difference in not filling up that 'pain' cup, which is inside, with more suffering and negative vibrations. I had been a receiver and a carrier of other people's traumas and tragedies as much as having my own grief and pain to look after. I learnt to live with it so well that it has become the most familiar and safe place for me to be. I understand pain, I know it. I can carry and hold a lot of it.

My dream last night demonstrated perfectly what is happening within and it shows progress and forward movement in my process. It is so striking that this image should come in with such clarity of presentation. My heart is in a cage, however, compared with last year when I could not feel, see or find my heart at all, I woke up trembling with my heart beating with immense force in my chest. I had to lie and absorb that movement for quite a while. It was one of those bittersweet experiences, in between joy and sorrow. Last year my heart was frozen, dead even and no amount of healing, meditating or going within would move it. Think 'Snow Queen', think all archetypes of the wounded Feminine, which was once soft, but has had to become hard to survive. It was incredibly painful just to be aware of the fact that the heart within me was not alive to the point I could not connect to it or feel it in my body. I learnt to use my intellect to connect with the knowing of its existence and vibration, therefore, through a cognitive understanding I could still function within the emotional realm, yet that disconnection from the physical and emotional bodies had been repeatedly 'heart-breaking'. To me heartbreak is not only when you feel your heart breaking into pieces and you experience the pain physically, but also, the even harsher tragedy of when you feel nothing at all and are unable to connect to what you know is there; when the heart is unreachable.

This time, in my dream my heart is alive and bleeding even though it is still locked in a cage. There is a piece of glass wedged in it just on the bottom. I cried tears of sorrow and joy at the same time, as at last, I felt, saw and experienced my heart again. In a dream it came in a cage. It is not liberated just yet, but at least it is alive and beating visually and on a sensory level. The sensation of it was similar to when you are about to scream and it is stuck in your throat or you see a hand putting a key towards a keyhole, yet you stop right before. It is like that. It is not yet coming out...

What came with the image is a message of how the process is likely to unfold. It will be done with love, softness, courage and seeing beauty in every single thing. It will be done through liberating it, finding that 'freedom' signature, not saving or rescuing it. It is waiting for that cage door to be ready to open by itself rather than forcing the lock or breaking the bars on the cage. Through giving and receiving love that cage door will begin to open. I will have to be with the bleeding of my own heart for a while, but it is a bittersweet sensation to me and I know this is necessary to connect with the flow of energy, which is now accessible again. Blood is a sign of life and rebirth and I can feel the new current of life radiating through me. Within that bleeding heart there is love, beauty, courage and strength."

Death and rebirth dream

"Lately my dreams are filled with things dying, bodies falling apart and fresh blood. There are recognisable themes of death and rebirth and the need to step into the new. It is time to be reborn into a new identity, into the 'now' identity. Blood in dreams, as in life, is life-giving. It is our base-line and an indication that we are living and breathing. It has a lovely vibration for me in my dreams and I welcome 'bleeding' dreams. I also got to know that scenes of death, bodies, funerals and all things associated with the ultimate end are ways of showing me that parts of myself, as they had been, need to 'die', renew and be reborn. In alchemy this process is called Motificatio.

Following death dreams there is always an appearance of things transforming and for me it is always associated with love and the alchemical marriage of the Feminine and Masculine. These are my absolute favourite dreams, because of how they feel. Incredible unconditional love surges through my body, as I sleep in deep enjoyment of that experience. Those dreams are often difficult to explain, or even express what they feel like, as they seem beautiful beyond words, otherworldly. They are truly an embodied experience of divine love, which we are part of. Nice to be reminded."

Through tracking dreams, we can be put in touch with our inner processes on a deep level and images presented to us in dreams can become navigational tools we can engage with on our spiritual journeys.

Symbols, images and archetypes in dreams

Symbols, images or archetypes from your dreams, particularly strong-feeling or repeating ones can be worked with in spell castings to improve a situation, as well as to clarify, understand and integrate something.

Some symbols are common and often come to all of us in

dreams, but a meaning will be specific to an individual, so go with your intuition when exploring your post-dream feelings to decipher it for yourself.

Dreaming of a house or a dwelling, for example, shows a state of our inner world at any given moment. I often dream of houses and depending on where I am in life that house image changes. In some dreams it is a derelict ruin and in others I am in magnificent palaces filled with space and gold. My inner world can be shown as a luxurious hotel, a palace, a tower in a castle; a small cottage or a flat.

* * *

One time I was in a perfectly formed, compact flat in an ancient building full of history and spirits. I remember touching its exposed old stone walls and feeling a sense of awe and joy of living in such a sacred place. I felt a sense of legend, wise men and education surrounding me. I had to climb to the dwelling through dark and narrow corridors till I reached the flat I was to call my home and when I made it inside and came up to an open window, I saw the whole world right in front of me. I could see for miles and the horizon spread in front of me filled with beautiful golden light. It felt magnificent and my heart sang with gratitude and peace. This represented a few things unique to my inner state at the time of this dream.

* * *

I had this dream before Yule. A Masculine energy dream. There was a man in my dream, who wanted me to draw a symbol in the air with my hand. He was giving me instructions on how to do it and I managed to produce one after several attempts.

Meaning: movement, work, growth.

Uruz: (U: Auroch, a wild ox.) Physical strength and speed, untamed potential. A time of great energy and health. Freedom, energy, action, courage, strength, tenacity, understanding, wisdom. Sudden or unexpected changes (usually for the better). Sexual desire, masculine potency. The shaping of power and pattern, formulation of the self.
Source: (sunnyway.com)

This dream, to me, strongly speaks of the presence of Masculine energy within me at that time and how aligned it was with the current season before the Oak king is born again into light on the 21st December. This energy is familiar to me and one of great achievements and productivity.

For me winter time is when my inner world forms into a whole. Masculine and Feminine merge together, and shows me how Masculine energy is often misunderstood and misinterpreted. There are stereotypes of what a man or a woman should be, what qualities they should portray and which they should hide. My dreams often show me how to break through those stereotypes and look within for what it means for me and what is of value to me at the time. The man in my dream was not perfect, was not strong or "together", if anything he was a bit lost, unsuccessful yet holding his head high and opening his big heart. His voice was gentle, not booming and strong, full of offering support and encouraging me to make my own choices. It keeps the door open for me, invites me to step into my own "masculine" qualities whatever that might mean for me. I have to spend some time after such dreams in quiet contemplation to make sure I really hear him with no judgement.

* * *

I had a dream once, which strongly connected me to the Crone aspect of myself. A Feminine energy dream. I felt this incredible power deep inside my being and a sense of anything being possible in all terms; shadow and light, destroy and flourish, love and force, revenge and forgiveness, anger and surrender.

The dream sparked my strong association with the crone Goddess Baba Yaga. It revealed my connection with her qualities. She was very much a part of me. I spent my day in contemplation of what it meant for me and, of course, messages became clear pointing me towards certain qualities that I had within me, which the Crone planted into my soul. It also pointed towards my past wounds, which I had suppressed and buried. It was time I looked at it fully. It was always inevitable and I had known that it would surface. The material I had been avoiding was rich with valuable lessons and ultimately was seeking to help me become a fully integrated person. It had been a long time coming and I felt in love with the process of unfolding through the imagery and stirrings in my soul that the dream offered.

Remember, in dreams what matters very much is how they make you feel. Your emotions and after-dream states are pointers towards what is to be learnt and what to pay attention to. The feelings that one wakes up with in the morning after a powerful dream cannot be made up. It is potent, it is there and it is leading us to where we are meant to be going in terms of manifesting our own qualities into our daily lives, decoding symbols and messages and making sense of what it is like to be us, to be fully conscious of the paradigms and realities we find ourselves in.

Dreams offer very rich material to us in terms of what we need to integrate, embrace, celebrate and learn about ourselves. Dreams are great tools in our quest for self-realisation, for individuation. If one is fully conscious of dreams' potentialities and possibilities, one will be welcomed into the potent world of significant symbols and sensations, which ultimately lead us to the core of ourselves. This is invaluable when we are developing and exploring a spiritual path and looking to practice magic using ourselves as much as intuitive method does.

Exercises

- Let go of any rules or attachments to a particular meaning of dreams.
- Follow your felt sense, ask yourself first and foremost "how did I feel when this and that happened?" when reflecting on a dream.
- How did I feel when I woke up?
- Was there a particular image, figure, character, colour or space that struck you in a
- Was there a feeling or sensation you were left with for hours after waking?
- Recall any sudden changes in feelings, scenery or behaviour. How did that feel?
- If you get an insight into what a dream might mean, do not rush, sit with it and unpack it bit by bit.
- Just know that whatever makes sense to you is the right way to go about interpreting and integrating dreams' material.

Intuitive Witch's tip

All dreams are about YOU and FOR you.

Chapter 3

Intuition and Working with others

At the centre of my work is intuition. It is my navigation system that allows me to relate and understand myself and others on a deeper level. Energies go through me and reflect back to whoever is being with me; whatever I might be working with, and it is that *"going through me"* technique that allows me to know what the other might need and benefit from.

Intuition is also used in "magical" workings and 90% of my magic/spiritual work is intuitive and always has been from the very beginning when I stepped onto the nature-based spiritual path. It is an exciting journey and I never once doubted what I do. There is not often right or wrong there is only better or poorer adjustments to what's available. Some work can be intense and alignment is stronger and in other cases it is less so and effects are subtler. Intuition is something to be trusted and to be open to and I am completely and utterly in its power knowing it will lead me where I need to go. It offers a well of possibilities of your own self-knowledge. All the treasure is already within us and one way to access that treasure is through intuition and listening to your inner voice of wisdom.

As an Integrative transpersonal psychotherapist and a magic practitioner, I use myself and my intuition to decide, and most of the time know what's needed, when, how and for who. Because intuition is based on feelings and sensations it makes me feel very connected to my own emotional states and those of others. It amplifies and zooms in on my quality of empathy. I pick techniques, approaches and a line to follow from my collection of tools, knowledge and experience through listening to the other's story and working cognitively, emotionally and spiritually, using my body and being aware of the energy that is present. I use my whole self to inform me of the needs of a client. It is deeply relational, on a soul level, one might say, when myself and the other operate as one, as two humans on a journey of discovery. I work as a guide, support system, safe space and a container for the other person while they go through a process of transformation. There is no judgement and we work with an open heart, unconditional love and acceptance.

Magic is involved in psychotherapeutic work. There are often moments of connection and insight in a therapy room, which feel truly magical. Psychologists also call it transpersonal experiences. Many of my colleagues would agree. It is the same in my work with the elements and nature, talking to trees, creating rituals and spells, working with deities. "Magic" in both contexts means moments of divine connection when forces align and energies peak or flow in a certain way that makes manifestation, healing and transformation possible. Results occur as a consequence of a way of working that is deeply spiritual and earthly at the same time. It is rooted in love and related through the heart.

I am truly appreciative of how parts of myself align into one purpose whether I am being a therapist or a nature adventurer, ritual creator or a spiritual guide. It feels incredibly rich and immensely fulfilling. I can find magic all around me and I look forward to continuing my work with intuition as my guiding force and constant companion.

Developing and working with intuition over time can increase empathy and through empathy a connection with others and the world at large will grow. You will begin not just noticing a cut tree or a hole in a trunk or a bird with a broken wing you will feel the others' pain and place in the wider system where all is connected and all beings feel similar things. Nature as a whole will then open itself up to a deeper relationship with everything and everyone. I am not talking of personification of nature necessarily, but an idea that everything is sentient and worthy of care and consideration. A living organism that is not necessarily something person-like, but a living energy body with its own cycles, struggles and challenges and zest for life.

I am hoping to introduce you to these ideas so that you might feel you want to go and explore it further and find ways of relating it to your practice, deepening it in whatever way that resonates.

Exercises

- Next time someone talks to you, see if you can focus on not just listening, but seeing and feel into the other person's reality. Imagine you are in their situation, in their shoes, as they say. What would you do and how would you feel?
- Notice if any insights about life, yourself, the world, and the other person that come into your awareness after actively listening to the other.

Chapter 4

Intuition and Journaling

Find a special journal/notebook or create one yourself for recording visualisations, drawings, dreams, important events, making general notes, writing your observations on feelings and experiences and, of course, for recording your spells. This journal will be your companion on your sacred journey of building your intuitive practice.

Why not choose your journal intuitively? When you go shopping notice what draws your attention and reflect on why that might be. Explore what it might mean and what it says about you. Write it down in the journal.

You can introduce curiosity and creativity to the process of choosing your journal and how you are going to use it. May be you will want to have several? Listen to that voice when you stand in front of a display of journals in the shop. Once you have it and bring it home with you, again spend time holding it and see what comes to you.

I have been keeping a journal since I was a child. I have never been without one. It allowed me not just record what was important to me, but to use it in various ways, for example, thoughts that would often come intuitively got turned into poems or even prose later on in life. I also always knew where that "line / sentence" was stored whenever I needed it for a project. There will always be a link, a memory leading me just to the right place. Once I went on a journey for the whole year with my journal and looked at it on a month-by-month basis. That was one of the most satisfying experiences I have ever had with journaling and recording. I called it a tool for raising self-awareness. To be spiritually aware what can be more important than self-awareness? Being self-aware puts you directly in the present, in the body and offers options and choices for how to proceed or look or think about something. Self-awareness is invaluable in magic spiritual practice. You have got to know yourself and recognise the sound of your own intuition speaking. To be able to discern messages from what some call "unconscious" or "intuitive knowing" you have got to understand yourself, what your limitations and triggers are, what your strengths and weaknesses, sweet points and edges are. You must be able to say a clear "yes" or "no" to yourself and others. Journaling is one tool that works to bring some illumination to what your reality is at any given time. I recommend keeping a journal to everyone and the feedback and results that come from that practice are huge and revelatory. It can also be sobering and grounding, which leads to quick and more permanent changes.

I provide details on the experience below recorded at the time:

Example

In 2018 I went on a journey of tuning into myself and the world around me on a month-by-month basis with nature continuing to be my sacred, supportive and grounding space. It was an incredible way of getting to know myself. I was not just surprised but amazed at various things that I didn't even know existed.

I took an approach of keeping a journal taking one month at a time. Focusing my awareness of what happens within me at any given moment, things that arise when engaging with people and partaking in events or when being silent or walking in nature. Feelings that come up for me spontaneously and consciously, when in the here and now, when asleep, and through dream observations.

The main aim of the exercise was to sharpen my self-awareness in terms of qualities, strengths, weaker points, triggers, ways of relating, preferences in being, how well-balanced or unbalanced something was within and tuning into needs that were either always met or never met. These are just some examples of this practice. My focus was to be on myself and then on the overall spiritual practice that I have built and life in general. I wanted to gain insights into what works and what doesn't.

Here's a list of qualities I have discovered and zoomed in to for each month as I became aware of those energies in me. Just to give you an example and yes, a lot of it surprised me and offered and opportunity for change.

Once we become aware of something, we are then offered a choice. We can choose what we do with that newly found information. That's a beauty of making the unconscious conscious. You can go as deep as you wish into what you discover, or observe it simply as it is or both.

January: "I have truly experienced myself as 'nice'. This might sound strange (it was to me), but I saw just how divorced I have been from myself in that sense and what it meant. I could never quite catch or understand what being 'nice' meant when people would so often refer to it in very general terms. I believe generalisation is a problem, just like the word 'fine', for example. I took 'nice' as a basis for what I was discovering and dived deeper. The difference was that this time I truly felt the quality in my body, which I could call a quality of softness, gentleness, kindness, all of it mixed together. This time I really knew that to be true. Beautiful sensation. How I could use it had no limits, as once I knew something was in my body and I had that experience of really feeling and being with something, I discovered I could always come back to it over and over. It has been useful particularly in creating rituals and spell-working with the Water element and the Goddess archetype. It could also be used in healing."

February: "I spent most of the month in a state of light and loving kindness. It was all about love, the pure and transcendent kind. Another beautiful state. I was made aware that I was able to go to that place a lot easier than I have given myself credit for in the past."

March: "I was able to transform my relationship with physical pain and learnt to listen to it."

And so it goes on. Each month there was a theme or a feeling that would centre on me and ask for attention and I would journal around what came up daily. I had an incredible year overall as a result of this practice and partly that was due to my conscious decision to be aware at all times and in tune with what arose without trying to fight it or change it. I observed myself and wrote about it.

At the end of the calendar year I was full of lessons and knowing, more than I did the year previously. My experiment in conscious transformation work and active personal evolving was very rewarding and highly interesting. I would recommend this self-awareness tool to everyone looking to dive deeper into finding out more about themselves including the much subtler layers of psyche, not just things that might be familiar or obvious. Super fun. Writing as a tool is generally transformative and healing. If you enjoy writing this one won't disappoint.

This is something I think I will always continue doing in one form or another. Remaining in wonder and in a state of enchantment, is an essential part of life and spiritual practice to me and as long as awareness is there, life is full of all things interesting.

Exercises

- Can you come up with a creative activity that can help with self-awareness?
- Take notes, keep a journal.

Chapter 5

Intuition and Sacred space

Explore your house looking for a place/s you feel most relaxed and comfortable in. It might be the whole room or a particular corner in a room. Explore the energy of that space when you find it, tune into it and raise that same vibration within yourself. Sit still in your chosen space absorbing its vibrations. As your next step you might want to create an altar in the space you most resonate with for working your magic.

You will have an answer about what you need to do specifically once you find that space. Follow your inner guidance. If you receive a message to create an altar, you will also have a feeling for what sort of items you might want to display there, e.g. candles, flowers, crystals, tree bark or leaves, jewellery, particular objects, Tarot cards or anything that has special meaning for you. Play with it and listen to that inner voice guiding you.

There are no rules here and it can be quite fun doing these exercises, which put you in touch with your intuition and working with vibrations. Creating an altar indoors is not compulsory, as magic done outside can be more appealing, however, for many (myself included) it is a combination of the two, working inside and outside, that work best.

The same method applies to looking for a special outside place. Do you live near a river, woods, a park or mountains? Is there a specific place you are drawn to?

Explore and find a spot you enjoy being in. For example, I have a tiny room in my house (also my office) where I do my magic on the floor. I like small spaces. They make me feel cosy and contained. I don't have an altar in that room, but I have a small altar in my bedroom, which I change whenever I am called to and for each magical holiday according to the Wheel of the year. Another space I have is in one corner of my garden, which I knew was special straight away as soon as I walked past it many years ago.

I found a few magical objects buried in that corner as years went by, including my cauldron.

One more place for me is in the woodlands across the road from where I live. There are three particular trees I talk to and have built a relationship with over the years. There is also a little stream in the woodland where I go to do my water magic sometimes. There are as many variations as there are beings. The main thing here is the joy of exploring and creating something personal through tapping into what vibrates the highest and shines the brightest for you.

Exercise

- Explore your home and your immediate surroundings outside. Is there a particular place you are drawn to? Is it near or far? Is it a tree, a river, an opening in the woods, a particular street, a park or a specific corner in your home?

Chapter 6

Intuition and Breathing

In magic breathing correctly is a number one tool to help you enter into a state of relaxation and receiving. In order to meditate and visualise correctly you must learn to breathe correctly. When exercising breathing there is also a chance to discover more of your own elemental nature, e.g. which element you might resonate most strongly with.

You might not be aware, but through exploring the Elements' breaths (below), it will be revealed to you.

For breathing exercises assume a comfortable position in your sacred space, either by sitting down or lying down or anything else that is comfortable for you and focus on breathing deeply involving your diaphragm and filling your lungs with air. Relax your body and inhale through your nose filling up your lungs to the count of three, four or five. Hold it for a few seconds and release through your mouth. Never go passed the level of comfort. Perform this several times holding your attention on your breath and the physical experience of breathing.

Elements' breathing can also correspond (if you wish to do so) to the Elements you choose to work with in your spells (more on spells and Elements later on). For now, go ahead and explore the Elements' breaths and see what you find most comfortable. Water breath is the most common (in through your nose, out through your mouth).

Elements' breaths

As you breathe visualise each element, e.g. while doing the Earth breath (inhale nose/exhale nose), visualise yourself either sitting or lying on the ground, grass, sand or walking barefoot in mud or being under the ground. Observe what that feels like to you. Do you enjoy it or do you reject/resist it? Is it a nice sensation or is it uncomfortable?

While doing the Fire breath (inhale mouth/exhale nose), imagine yourself surrounded by fire, being on fire or jumping through or above fire. What do you feel? Is it a nice sensation or do you want to stop?

For Water (inhale nose/exhale mouth) imagine swimming or being on top or under water. For Air breathing (inhale mouth/exhale mouth) imagine flying like a bird taking in the overall view. Is it scary or is it freeing?

Once you've gone through all the breaths use your journal to make notes or draw a picture/s of all of your experiences. Having a visual can be very revealing and tell a story you might not have been aware of.

I have given you here a system of breathing, but why not go further and use your intuition regarding breathing and the Elements? You can use images that come up when you think of an element. You might feel a certain way that then makes you want to breathe a certain way. To get in touch with the elements you can go out in in heat of the summer; climb and sit upon a mountain in windy conditions; lie on the ground or work with soil, e.g. planting or you can try swimming or sitting by a body of water. With each element discover for yourself in which direction energy flows. Is it up, down, vertical, horizontal, none of the above or all of the above? Experiment.

Exercise

- Revisit the Elements' breaths regularly to get in touch with their energies. Practice breathing and exploring them.

Chapter 7

Intuition and Creative Imagination

This is an important technique in any magical practice. It is also sometimes called journeying, and is a powerful magical tool to create what you want in your mind's eye and enter a space where your inner voice is heard. You could think of it as setting your intention on what your desired outcome is to be. This is a very important technique to practice every day if you are to advance in your intuitive magic practice.

Start by finding a position that is comfortable for you, where you will be relaxed, and which you can hold for some time. Begin with your breathing and use it to enter a state of relaxation and imagine what you wish to create. Hold the image firmly in your focus, observe it, notice what it looks and feels like, e.g. a healed wound or a soul mate walking towards you, or receiving a letter with good news.

The focus is on pure heart and gratitude. For example, when thinking of money the focus should always be on abundance and gratitude for what you already have rather than on what you feel you are lacking. When performing a prosperity or money spell you are advised to focus on inviting more into your life, spelling out your specific needs and asking for help to create more abundance in your life.

Visualisation is a way to raise your energy and focus on something you wish to manifest.

I like to use drawings after a visualisation, but you might feel you don't need to, so do whatever you feel is right for you, you will know what that is once you come out of a visualisation. I often use drawings in spells, which are born through visualisations. I will expand on this method later.

Exercise

- Explore ways your intuition and creativity meet and how you like to visualise things.

Chapter 8

Intuition, Trust and Ethics

Once you learn to trust yourself you will know that you are doing the right thing. There is psychology behind this and can be healing. Perhaps, historically, self-esteem and confidence have been knocked or self-value has not been reflected back. This way of working, trusting your intuition, can empower you and put you in touch with the qualities that have always been within you and can now freely come forward and make your world and the world of others shine again.

There are a few things in any acquired or discovered magical practice that one must know, that we apply to when and how we practice, which should be considered. Integrity and ethics are two of those things. Trust that your intuition will not lead you onto a path that lacks integrity or is unethical. I refer later on in this book to the importance of giving thanks and doing everything from the heart centre, but another aspect of magic is that it should really be the last "go to practice"; the last step especially when it comes to certain aspects. A good example of this would be health. Magic does not replace a good advice from a healthcare practitioner. This is something I have discovered for myself through intuitive guidance and it has formed my ethical framework, if you like, for my practice.

Magic is very powerful and because of that if misused or not handled with care, it can also be very damaging and spiral out of control, involving yourself and sometimes even others. Correct understanding, practice and application is required. In cases of doubt or an impulse to do something you know deep down might not be right intuition can be invaluable. Its feeling function or purpose will tell you what is what, just by making you feel a certain way. This is not about what you are capable of doing potentially to bring on a desired change, but how and when you do it. Magic demands respect! It is a powerful tool and also a delicate thing that if abused will produce effects that are potent with unwanted results, which can be difficult and sometimes impossible to untangle.

My magical and spiritual practice confirmed it for me many times over by intuitively diverting me away from doing something I might have regretted later on or showing me what consequences might be if I were to rush into things. With that "warning" type of energetic exchange it also began teaching me how to use my intuition with regards to when and how to perform magic. Not only did this confirm that magic should always be the last resort, but that all circumstances, elements, and energies somehow need to be in a particular order, held in readiness to perform what is needed at the time.

I always use my intuition to know what to include, how to place items and in which order, as well as when to do it. I simply can't do it any other way now; it has become natural. You ARE your best tool, so to speak, and it is about holding the faith that you will know not just when to do something, but how to do it and what to use.

Before jumping into the cauldron and starting to cook up your spells, so to speak, spend some time with the cauldron. I am using metaphor here to demonstrate how other things need to come in and be played around with and resolved before resorting to some magical doing. However, there are, of course, exceptions when magic can be an additional tool to a mixture of approaches you would like to use. Magic can enhance a particular experience or increase your productivity in doing something. It can also serve as a tool that "seals the deal", which acts as the last grounding effect of energy you have been working with in other modalities; be it expressing yourself through art, healing with herbs, checking things out with a doctor, if it is a health issue, or talking to people, having therapy sessions and using your own creative imagination to access your higher self for answers. Whatever it might be magic spells can be added to the mixture to complete a piece of work. This is something I do and it feels very grounding. What I don't do is decide to do a healing spell, as the first call, or do a love spell when something is out of alignment within me without addressing the relationship/s in question. I have an understanding that some things not only will not work, but that it can make it worse if done unconsciously and without due care.

When people come to me with questions and magic requests I always provide them with a list of things they could consider doing before involving some magical workings. I do my work with an empowerment message at the centre and provide suggestions relevant to the situation someone is bringing as well as shining a light on their potential, getting them to connect to themselves on a level that will facilitate that process of resolving something. I also do not produce magic spells for other people, but I do encourage them to create their own by tapping into their magical resources and potential. I might give suggestions for ingredients they could look into, but ultimately what they put into their work is their responsibility and it is a privilege to assist people in working with their own power.

Here is an example when neither help from outside nor a specific spell was needed for me to achieve a resolution.

Example

There is nothing like spring coming back that invites us more into life. It calls for awakening from the stillness and dreaming of dark winter. It pulls a body into a much-needed stretch, into a new kind of movement and engagement with the world. It offers that space to hear a new song from within ourselves that had been hibernating in darkness.

Winter can be a tough time for many, a time that makes us feel stuck in chaos, confused and stalled, with not much movement present other than in dreams. This process is necessary, as everything always is, and the purpose of the "stuckness" is to explore ourselves from a position of where we are and who we are; what our realities are and whether they serve us. It is not an easy path to understand and integrate, however, relying on intuition and instinct is useful. There is nothing wrong with asking for help from outside when we are stuck and this can be particularly useful and necessary for those of us, who are not used to asking for help and instead there for everyone else. This could be healing. The work for me during a particular winter was to get to know that pattern again from the perspective that actually it is completely okay to ask for that hand that we need to hold on to and it is okay not to lead for once. I also realised that when we do ask for help, we are then able to help ourselves better – an interesting insight, which manifested through some magical workings that also involved asking for help from the Elementals, in this particular example. This is something I had not done before quite in this way, but, as always based on the intuitive knowing, this is what came through at this time.

I asked "Help me" while walking in nature and two days later I got it. It came as a voice, a message, an insight that said "Help yourself". It contained the energy of giving back to me the knowing and responsibility for my own healing. It was nice to have that confirmed. We are the best healers for ourselves without a doubt, but that does depend very much on our relationships with ourselves. Doing the "self" work whether it is through a therapeutic relationship or a spiritual practice, puts you in touch with yourself like nothing else and that is the most important element to ensure one lives in a way that is "whole", fulfilling, and peaceful. Without a doubt the best gift of self-work is you integrating back into what you were always meant to be with all your beautiful resources, qualities, unique gifts, resilience and potential intact. In order to get there we often need to ask for help, we need to learn to reach out and relate, to connect without fear or judgement. We need to be vulnerable to become truly strong and grounded and we need courage and strength to be vulnerable when it is terrifying.

This inner spring already feels like a very nourished, turned-over soil that is ready to offer that space and wisdom to us for planting anew. We need to be patient with our newly planted seeds, warm and kind with ourselves, accepting of all that we are, good and bad, twisted and glorious, strong and weak. All of that richness is the soil of our bodies and the light of our souls. I am excited to see what is to come. It is all new again.

Exercises

- Become aware of how you feel through tuning into your inner voice and your body's sensations.
- Have a dialogue with the feeling you identify in whatever way feels right to you.
- Only proceed with your intentions and ensure when you feel sure.
- Consider "Harm no one" statement and what it means to you and how would you best avoid potentially causing harm to yourself and others?

Chapter 9

Intuition and Moon Cycles

In this chapter, like I do throughout the book, I encourage you to focus on your intuition. Continue listening to that inner voice and tapping into your inner knowing of what resonates the most with your highest self.

Intuition plays a major part in spell-working and I always work in the intuitive way doing things when I feel it is right and include only those elements, which align with the intention I have at the time.

Intuition also applies when working with the moon cycles in my practice. To give you an example, I very rarely do spells at Full Moon even though, as you might have heard, Full Moon is when the energy is at its highest and it is a great time for setting your intentions and working on your goals. However, during Full Moon my energy is highly strung, my mind is clouded and my emotions are often so raw that I find there is a great resistance to doing any magical work at this time. What I do instead is simply observe in quiet reflection. I have discovered this pattern, as I progressed in my practice. This is a good example of working intuitively and tapping into all aspects of my being: my thoughts, emotions and body.

When engaging with magical workings and something doesn't feel right for me and I can sense resistance I never force it regardless of what plans I might have made for that day.

This applies to all spells and all Moon cycles. Never perform a spell when you are in a negative thought pattern or in a low vibrational energetic state. Although I absolutely love the Moon's energy and being out in the Moonlight is the most pleasant sensory experience for me, performing spells during Full Moon is difficult. I enjoy having a quiet ritual simply by spending time with the Moon, but that's as far as I go. You see, the journey is very individual just as our energies are individual. There are similarities, but there are also many peculiarities and oddities, which only you can find out and experience.

The way to go is to find these things out for yourself and to do that you need to listen to your intuition, and pay attention to your body and your emotional and energetic vibrations during each Moon cycle.

Here is a quote I found from another magical worker, which confirms what I have just described to you.

> *"If you don't know what you want, resist the temptation to work magic under the Full Moon simply because it's a good time for magical workings. Instead, consider performing a ritual to honour the Goddess and feel as one with her. This can be a powerful enough experience on its own."*
> Source: a blog post *Magic and Moon Phases* by Charlie on October 22, 2014; http://community.humanityhealing.net/

The Moon is very important when working with magic. She represents the power of the feminine energy, the Lady Goddess, the energy of emotion, reflection and intuition.

Amazing things can happen as a result of Moon spells and rituals if you embrace the magic within you and align with the energy of nature.

Full Moon – make a wish your heart desires

The most powerful time for magic is when the energy is at its highest and most open (love and happiness spells, health and vitality, celebrating life in general with full power, protection, divination, money, dreams and anything to do with legal matters). At this time, you can ask the energy, the Moon, the Goddess (whichever resonates with you more) to assist you with anything in general.

New Moon – planting a seed

The day of the New Moon and three days following is the second most powerful cycle and I very much like the energy of the New Moon (beauty, health, job and business, protection, and new beginnings of any sorts generally). It is a powerful time to send your wishes and desires out into the Universe, focusing on what you wish for more of in your life with gratitude for what you already have, and so increasing whatever you are thankful for and what gives you joy already.

New Moon is also sometimes called Dark moon. It is a time for going within, for deep reflection on the "shadow" sides within yourself and on the outside, any negative emotions you might be holding. Really go deeper into understanding what they represent and mean to you and what lessons they carry. Everything has meaning and often in the darkest places you find the things, which mean a great deal.

Waning Moon – letting go

The time for releasing, cleansing, getting rid of what is not wanted, removing, banishing, eliminating and letting go of everything that no longer serves you (negative thoughts, clearing of spaces, sending away ill health, pain, etc.).

It is important to mention that when "sending things away" you should also pay attention to what the lessons have been for you in experiencing those things that you now wish to eliminate. Reflect on it and learn from it rather than setting an intention of rejecting something and tossing it out without meaning.

Waxing Moon – growth

This is the time for expansion, increasing, constructive magic, building on what you have started at the New Moon; the continuing growth of your goals and intentions, stimulating and growing and inviting what you wish for more of in your life (health, prosperity, love and friendship and strength).

New Moon Intuitive Spell examples

New Moon is a fantastic time to set your intentions for new goals, aspirations, relationships, projects and dreams. I suggest a couple of spells here, which have a very soothing, hope-filled vibration. Just as Full Moon is difficult for me, the New Moon time is my absolute favourite where I feel the most calm and peaceful. Your intuition will guide you to a specific Moon Cycle that will work for you:

Find an object inside or outside. It can be a stone, a twig, a leaf, some tree bark or a crystal anything that when you begin to focus on it comes into your physical awareness.

You will recognise it when you come across it. You can perform this in your chosen sacred space inside or outside or you can just sit wherever you are called to do it at the time.

Settle yourself comfortably, close your eyes and follow your breath (whichever type of breathing best suits you). When you feel that you have access to the "in-between thoughts" state paying a gentle attention to your breath and think of all the wonderful things that you already have and that you wish to have MORE of in your life. Declare that everything you think and feel is fully from your heart and from a space of unconditional love towards yourself and others. Think of qualities that you value in your experience and in people around you, which you would like to attract MORE into your life. Holding your chosen object in the palm of your hand, focus your attention and intention on "injecting" all the qualities you chose into the object and send your energy into it, e.g. generosity, kindness, good health, affection, tenderness, etc. The list can be as small or as big as you wish. You might want to be very specific with one or two things, or you can adopt a general "more of good vibration" approach with this spell. It is entirely up to you and you will know the path you will take once you set out working with it. When you finish putting all the goodness into your object find a spot outside where you will bury the object. Find a place where it is clean and joyous where you feel the energy is conducive to positive growth and expansion. Let it "grow" in the Earth, ask the Universe to make all of those things bigger and better with gratitude and love. And leave it there.

Here is a spring spell using herbs, cleavers in this case. Cleavers is a wonderful herb/weed, which contains many healing properties beneficial to the body. I have also been enjoying its "sticky" texture when working in the garden and on my allotment. When weeding I found that everything else sticks to it, and this makes for easy carrying and disposal. Fantastic. I love its appearance and texture. It is also a very playful herb in its energy. It is easily recognisable, widely available during spring/summer and simple to work with.

When walking in the woods on the eve of a New Moon doing some mindful healing and tree talk I was drawn to cleavers in the hedgerow. I decided to do a quick spell, a small creative piece to coincide with my favourite Moon cycle.

New Moon is all about starting over. It offers an opening for things to be planted. Taking cleavers off the hedges and gathering it in my hands I found myself making a "wish doll". I made a small body with a flower crown on top and as I was weaving cleavers round and round the figure I was naming things I would like to work on during the new cycle, wishing for things I would like to have more of in my life and inviting improvements to come in areas of my choice. I found myself smiling once I finished this quick spell and a feeling of loving comfort came over me. It felt just right to have done this. I left the doll amongst ivy wrapped around a hawthorn trunk asking for protection and growth.

You can come up with your own New Moon spell.

As the starting point for future New Moon spells, during your day or week think of something good in your life that you wish to expand on. Really focus on it, look at your intentions behind your wish and whether your motivations are based on an open heart and pure thought and how it makes you feel thinking about it, whatever it is. It is important to check it out against your felt sense in the body and what your intuition might say to you on the subject. Write some things down, journal your thoughts, intentions and feelings around it, look at it from all sides. As you grow in your practice these things will come easier and quicker, but initially it is worth exploring every angle and the most important part is to pay attention to how you feel. What are you experiencing? Is there any resistance or impatience? Do you feel your mood change or you feel stuck? This is all important on your journey to knowing yourself as a magic practitioner.

Something that will help you in this is a practice called GROUNDING, which I will be talking about in the next chapter.

Exercises

- Try noting Moon phases in your journal alongside how you feel about each. Which cycle do you feel at your best/ weakest/most active? When do things flow more naturally for you?
- Consider a New Moon spell with the next cycle. Use your intuition to create one.

Chapter 10

Intuition and Grounding

As something to help you and also as a very important practice when working with magic I give you something to explore and practice every day – GROUNDING! It will help you bring focus and solidity to your thoughts and ideas and will allow you to work with clear intention and solid footing. Grounding is the act of connecting to the Earth, becoming as one with the power she holds. This will assist you in your magical practice.

This exercise is magical in itself and extremely valuable. Write it down in your special journal and practice, practice, practice. Feel free to do variations on it; pay attention to your intuition and your visualisations and improvise as long as you connect to the Earth in one way or another.

There are many grounding exercises out there. This one is my favourite. It is a Tree Grounding Meditation, which I put my own stamp on with elements that have been informed by my intuition. First and, perhaps, most importantly to me I wanted to establish a relationship with a particular tree, which I knew would only strengthen my grounding practice. If you think of the earth, the roots and tops of the tree it represents a whole system, "a body", if you like. That means that this practice will incorporate all aspects of yourself and provide just the right kind of grounding needed. Second, every time I know I need grounding there is a specific feeling that comes up. It might be anxiety, apprehension, fear or uncertainty. In short, the kinds of emotions that tend to take us into our heads/minds and which we attempt to solve using logic. In cases like this I know I have to do the opposite and bring a feeling down, into my body. With the help of earth and my chosen tree I will seek to neutralise the feeling and transform it into an energy more conducive to the work I intend to do.

A tree I have established a relationship with over the years is a beech tree. This relationship then extended to trees neighbouring to the central tree. The big tree has a sitting platform in the form of roots extending outwards and I use it to sit on when grounding. The other tree contains three trunks coming out from one main root. I use this tree as a container for my grounding practice where I climb inside an opening in-between outstretched trunks and it feels like the tree holds me on all sides. The Meditation is as follows:

I either sit again a tree or stand inside a cluster of trees, as above, (if access to a tree is difficult or impossible for you, placing hands on a trunk or holding on to a branch are good alternatives) and start breathing slowly, bringing my attention fully to the present moment and my body. I become aware of inhaling and exhaling, experiencing every breath as my mind becomes quieter and quieter and I experience a sensation of lightness and softness. Then I imagine becoming a tree (any tree, imaginary or a one chosen by you), i.e. merging with its essence, texture and smell. Imagine you have roots growing down from your toes. First visualise your energy going down into the centre of the Earth (however you imagine that). I see a large ball of green energy. The roots hook to the centre of the Earth and pull the energy up into your body, the Earth energy (whatever that means to you and feels like). Breath in the energy as it goes up from the centre of the Earth through your roots into your body and breathe out any tension or worries that you might be holding back to the Earth. Earth transmutes and transforms all kind of energy, you can take and you can give back, it will always match whatever vibration is necessary. The Earth knows what to do. Continue visualising going down to the centre of the Earth with your roots, pulling the energy up and breathing out anything you want to let go of.

Other ways to ground include: walking barefoot, sitting on

the ground, hugging a tree, putting your hands into the soil or palms on the ground, eating root vegetables, placing grounding crystals around your home (haematite, tiger's eye, smoky quartz, red coral, onyx, black tourmaline, ruby, and garnet), burning incense or using essential oils with grounding properties, such as sandalwood, cedar, patchouli, and Ylang, Ylang or taking a salt bath using sea salt, Himalayan salt or Epsom salts. Grounding colours are reds, browns or blacks.

Please find some examples from my practice below.

Ever in doubt... ask a tree

One of my favourite practices that I have developed is communicating with trees. As I continued on my journey the link between my intuition, my feelings and externals sources of help and enhancements for my spiritual practice in nature, such as, trees, strengthened and I began intuitively recognising "a call" from, for example, a specific tree, a place, or an object. I found my questions often got answered by trees and I started visiting woods regularly to confirm things. I highly recommend trying this type of intuitive communication to ground emotions and get a perspective on whatever might come up for you on a specific day. Here is one experience:

One morning I was filled with anxiety and fear and I did not know the cause of it, but I knew it was trying to tell me something, as it always does. Remember intuitive connection often comes through feelings. I felt in great need to transmute the feelings, release and let them speak to me. I needed comfort, answers, reassurance and lessons, so I could take steps towards a goal I was intuitively setting myself. It felt big within my body. I was very aware of my breath and couldn't get enough air and this was so very symbolic of the thing that I was trying to release. This change, it felt, if it was implemented successfully would have a big impact on many factors within my reality and in the lives of others around me.

This morning I felt called to doing a particular spell. I wanted to write my own, but as I sat down with my magic journal it opened up on the page with the exact spell I needed to use. I decided to choose an incense to go with the spell and was drawn to sandalwood. As I sat down at my desk and lit a white candle fear and anxiety hit me. It was big and something I needed to sit with. I had all the ingredients and words ready yet I needed a confirmation of some kind, a sign, a reassuring nod, so I went to the woods to get clarity, to release some of the tension with the hope of coming back with a lighter load.

It was a wonderful walk and I experienced a harmonious tree talk. They all "nodded" to me in unison, which was such a lovely energetic and visual experience, from tall to short, huge to tiny, trees to shrubs, leaves to grass there was an orchestra of voices and movements as if to say to me "of course", "it is a yes", "go in peace".

There was an interesting symbolic representation of my sense of self and my relationship to myself and my body through various symbols I encountered on the walk. It was a riddle I had to work out, but that's the way I like it with nature. It often feels clear, but doesn't look clear, or vice versa. Sometimes it just simply hits you in the face with an insight. This time "house", "new" kept coming up. On my way I passed two houses, which in the past my family and I had looked at to move into. It caught my attention why it was so present for me this time when I had been on this walk hundreds of times before. There was something about a "house", a "new house". (Notice how intuitive imprints/messages came as images and specific words). Then I felt strong sensations in my body, something like being fully aware of my limbs, my bones, my skin and my whole structure. It felt wonderfully warm and reassuring. I loved being so in touch with my body and then it struck me, "house", "body", "new" – it all came together. It was referring to a "container", "a sense of self", a physical vessel, in which soul resides. It made sense to me what the message was and, of course, it was very closely linked to my initial question when I stepped into the woods.

The feelings from that experience turned out to stretch wider and carried a lot more power that I initially thought. Fear really gripped me in the evening in my solar plexus specifically. I have never felt a localisation of an emotion so strongly before. The next morning there was nowhere to run, as my stomach tightened so much my breathing became constricted.

What I wanted to demonstrate with this example was the intuitive way of living your life and being conscious of your emotions, body and what it all means for you in the present moment. The more you practice this way of being, the more natural it becomes and the more healing and joy you will invite into your life.

Lessons to share:

- Move your body in a loving and conscious way, honour and respect your body.
- Stop abandoning yourself and your body when things get tough, do not fly right out of it.
- Stop "leaving" and walking away and STAY present. This is incredibly freeing and healing.
- Whatever tension is in the body, first, be with it fully and unconditionally and then release in a way that feels right to you whether it is going for a run, take a swim, sit in meditation, do yoga or make love.

I mentioned using tools while I related my experience above. The important thing is that they feel right to you. It is my experience and example. I will be going more in depth about choosing and using tools in the next chapter.

Tools to use:

- Use a particular music you might associate with how you are feeling in the moment.
- Use colours, images and/or crystals that speak to you in that moment.

Exercise

- Practice grounding techniques (see if your own unique way shows itself) and start sourcing grounding stones/ crystals of your choice and resonance.

Intuitive Witch's Tips

- Never set an intention on hurting anyone.
- Never work in a low vibration or a negative mood.

Chapter 11

Selecting Tools Intuitively

Magic is deeply rooted in nature. From the Earth we come and to the Earth we return. It has powers to transmute any energy and return it to the original source or to wherever it is needed the most. To give you an example, here is a quick tip for you:

If at any point you feel negative influences around you, for example, if you are in a healing profession and you feel like you might have taken on some energy, which doesn't align with your higher self and it is dragging you down, there are some things you can do. You might want to find a crystal bracelet or a necklace to wear when you are around your clients, out in a social situation or in a crowded place. It can also be a shawl or a scarf that you wear around your neck and/or cover your chest if that is where your body absorbs energy. You might want to choose a protective stone or a specific object for yourself that can fit in a pocket or your bag. What crystals do is absorb any unwelcomed energy and there will come a point when it might be a good idea to cleanse them. That's where the element of Earth comes in.

Earth is the master transformer of energies and you can safely trust its natural powers to transmute and return all kinds of energy to where it is meant to go. You can cleanse low vibration objects that might feel like they carry unwelcomed energy by burying them in the Earth. Leave it in the ground overnight or even for a few days, whatever feels right for you. There are some exceptions to this, as not all objects will be suitable or small enough to do that with. In those cases, using water always works.

Magic to me is more of an art form than an exact science, although there are some general observations and rules, if you like, which are in alignment with scientific knowing. I follow my intuition and it is not necessarily fixed and, as previously discussed, if something doesn't resonate with me, I don't do it. I always follow my own calling to do things a certain way.

Forcing something always goes against what you are meant to be doing. For me magic is intuitive, flexible, and fluid rather than regimented, prescribed and rigid. Nobody's way of working magic is the same.

Your inner voice must align with your intentions and the energy that you would like to manifest into your reality. You might notice, as you progress through your own journey towards your inner magic that my practice might differ from others and that is okay. We are all individual and unique and I encourage you to find your own way. If there was only one piece of advice I was ever to give you it is this; never ever abandon your own voice! My magic is also simple, which means I don't use a lot of complicated rules or tools. I do whatever I am called to do, usually in a very simple way.

Elements are naturally present in nature and carry energies or signatures, which we can tap into, manipulate and work with to direct them towards our goals. Each Element traditionally corresponds to the four directions: North, South, East and West if you would like to use directions in setting up your magical working space or a ritual. You might feel you don't need to do that. I like to have a visual for directions, which I represent with crystals when working in my circle. Choosing crystals can be done intuitively by sitting with each Element at a time (or if you relate to directions better, use that), just like you did in your Elements breathing exercise, and see what colour you associate with each element and what stone you might choose to represent it. Whatever you choose will be right for you. Trust yourself to make the right choice and go fully with your intuition on this.

The way I chose mine when first starting out was not through the crystals' qualities and what they might mean, but simply by going with their vibrations and colours for each element, e.g. blue for Water, green for Earth, red for Fire and white/ translucent (Selenite, e.g.) for Air. If later you want to look into why you chose what you chose, you can do so and I am sure that every single element will make sense and every single crystal you chose to represent your elements will correspond with your intention, if you truly and deeply listened to your inner voice. It can be very revealing.

Casting a circle

Once you have all your materials ready you can cast a circle. You can call in The God, The Goddess and all the Elements or nothing and no one. You can use a silver candle for the Goddess and a golden one for the God.

In your sacred place using visualisation and breathing start walking nine times around, which is a traditional option (or whatever is being said for you to do by your intuition) or simply draw a circle around yourself with Athame like I do (a knife reserved for magic and ceremonial work). Ensure all your items are already in the circle.

You may choose to oil and dress a candle/s (instructions for dressing a candle can be found later on in the book), if you choose to work with a candle, you can do this before casting a circle or do it once you finished casting it. I do it beforehand.

Then place all your items within the circle. Pay particular attention to the Elements, which correspond to the spell you are performing. Light your oiled candle (if using one), place it in the middle and visualise your intention and your wishes manifesting holding love and gratitude in your heart at all times.

As an example, this is how I lay out my circle for a healing spell. You can use this layout if you want, or play with it and find your own way.

There is a crystal in each of the directions' corners (North, South, East and West). The fifth direction on top of a pentagram represents a spiritual realm and for this I use Amethyst.

I also sometimes light a silver candle for the Goddess and sometimes I don't. You will know what is right for you. I use a flower in this particular spell and there is a chalice (silver in this instance) with some water in it. In the centre there is a white candle for healing and there are other crystals scattered around. In this instance I spell work in my sacred space. The circle is cast on an altar cloth with a pentagram on it. This is just to give you a visual idea of how it can be presented. Each element is representative of a set of qualities:

Water – emotional body, realm, field, whatever you want to relate to. Water is all about our emotions. The element holds vibrations of the following qualities: creativity, generosity, nurture, affection, empathy, compassion, devotion and grace. It holds a strong feminine vibration and corresponds to the Goddess and the Moon.

Fire – our energetic body. Fire holds the qualities of radiance, enthusiasm, passion, determination, perseverance, success, courage and strength. It corresponds to the Sun, the God and of masculine energy.

Air – our mind, cognition, thinking realm. Air holds vibrations of the following qualities: wisdom, intellect, wit, inspiration, knowledge, perception, insight, intuition and communication.

Earth – corresponds to focus and will, all things material and physical. Earth carries vibrations of the following qualities: strong will, organisation, focus, discipline, capability, pragmatism, firmness, trust, loyalty, patience, helpfulness, calmness, nobility, responsibility, and dependability.

As you set up your circle, invite elements in and sit with each of them in turn and then light your candle. Candles come in different colours and used for different spells. Each colour will correspond to your goal or intention; choose according to your intuition. White candles can be used in all spells (small ones, 4" long, are perfect for spell work). I shall be expanding on the magical uses of candles in the next chapter.

Exercises

- Experiment with ways of casting a circle. Do you like to do it indoors or outdoors?
- Do you like to walk your circle or draw it with a finger, feather, stick or knife? Do you prefer to visualise it instead?
- What tools appeal to you when setting up a circle?
- How would you close your circle?

Chapter 12

Intuition and Candle Magic

Some traditional, widely recognised and used associations and correspondences when working with candles are, as follows:

Abundance/money/wealth: green, copper, gold.
Banishing negativity: black, white, purple.
Success: red, purple.
Love: red, pink, white.
Employment: orange, brown.
Luck: orange, silver, yellow.
Peace: white, pink, black.
Cleansing: white.

If for whatever reason you are missing a specific colour of candle at the time of needing to perform a spell, use a white candle. It works with all spells and is a good all-around substitute.

I invite you to explore the given colours in more detail and see what resonates. Some spells require candles to be burnt for several days. In other spells a single candle is burnt until it is done. I have used candles in my magical workings from the beginning of my journey and usually do spells with small candles, which do not take a long time to burn out. You might choose your candles by colour, size, shape or vibration. Your intuition is the most important tool in figuring out how you want to choose your candles. I myself never refer to a prescribed candle magic practice and most of the time the suggested colours would not resonate with me, but it may for others depending on a specific magical set-up or intention. I use small white candles a lot in general. Perhaps, it is because I frequently work outside and small candles are more portable and quick to burn, but it may be that simplicity is always at the centre of everything I do and this is no exception. It has always been interesting to me how there is never any doubt or uncertainty in what I need to work with. My intuition is always there when it comes to specific methods of magic. Try it for yourself.

Dressing a candle

Dressing a candle means anointing it with oil. This step in candle magic is again optional. There have been times when I have found that the intuitive instructions I received were very specific with the exact name of the essential oil and the way to use it with a chosen candle. Use your intuition and, perhaps, a sense of smell and whatever you are drawn to at the time of performing your spell or a ritual. It is best to have all items to be used in a spell or a ritual ready before you start your magical working, as previously mentioned. It is just easier overall. You might 'be told' to use just one item or quite a few. It is never the same in my experience. An easy way to start is by following the steps below:

- Select a goal.
- Visualise the desired outcome.
- Select your tools according to your intuitive messages: candles, oils, crystals, herbs, etc.

Oils can be rubbed on a candle for a particular goal for spell-work. There are prescribed practices for this, which you might or might not find useful. Sometimes those practices will make sense and be in line with what you are looking to bring into the world, and at other times your intuition will tell you exactly what you need to do or use and it will be entirely different from the traditional rules. Trust your intuition.

Traditional methods of candle dressing

To simply dress a candle start rubbing the oil onto the candle from the centre to either end of the candle – Full Moon correspondence.

To draw something you want to invite more of into your life start at the top and move to the bottom of the candle – Waxing moon correspondence.

To banish, release or let go of something start at the bottom of the candle and move to the top – Waning moon correspondence.

Remember it is okay to come up with your own intuitive wisdom on working with candles and oils. Keep it simple, listen to your inner voice and always work with integrity and an open heart.

In place of oils or in addition to dressing your candles with oils you can burn an incense while performing a spell. The choice is again yours.

Peace Spell

Suggested ingredients:

Full Moon
A white candle
Elements of Air and Water
Lavender Oil to be dressed from the centre either way according to the Full Moon correspondence

I used my Athame to cast my circle and placed crystals in each direction corner. You can select your own, which you are drawn to in your association with each element. Air and Water are the main elements for this spell, so I have incense for Air and a small bowl of water for the Water element corner. My candle is oiled and lit and once this is done, I sit quietly in a visualisation in order to set my intention quietly and focus on my goal. I stay here as long as it feels right, keeping my focus.

Afterwards I close the circle by moving my Athame in the opposite direction nine times or walking in the other direction nine times (remember to follow your intuition here). I thank each deity for assisting me in my work: the Elements, The God and the Goddess.

Let your candle burn out. (You can get on with other things while the candle burns) Dispose safely either by wrapping it up and throwing out in the trash or returning to the Earth by burying it.

Intuitive Healing Spell

I would like to share one of my healing spells. I share this as an example of working with magic intuitively. Every element of the spell has been constructed through listening to my own intuition. This is very different to using a spell one would find in a book or on the internet. I always find constructing my own spells to be more powerful. This process is what this book is all about: to encourage and inspire you to find your own way towards your inner magic using your intuition as a guiding tool.

No one spell is the same for me. It makes it exciting. I tune into the emotional and physical state that I am in at the time and so there will always be different things resonating. One time it might be the Water spell, another time it might be the Earth element. This is what it makes it so joyous; experimenting and tuning into all the energies around you at the time and constructing something unique and specific using your inner wisdom and guidance. It keeps your magical practice truly grounded in the present moment.

For this spell I used:

- A white candle (you can also use green)
- A bowl of water with lemon and basil (I used a blue coloured bowl)

- A feather or a white flower
- Crystals (rose and clear quartz)

Ensure that all the ingredients are clean and that the flower/ herb/plant, if you are using one, is not harmful. This is a spell that involves ingesting the water at the end, so you need to know what you are putting into it.

To me this spell is intuitively a Water spell. However, if this doesn't resonate explore the Elements again and see which qualities align the most with your intention for this spell. Qualities I associate with Water are of healing and soothing quality, such as, softness and nurture. When I first did this I intuitively knew I had to incorporate a bowl of water.

This spell is best done during the Waning Moon (refer to the Chapter 9: Intuition and Moon Cycles). What I am trying to achieve here is to release some physical pain and heal a physical wound. This spell can also be done with emotional pain. On this occasion we will focus on a physical ailment to aid healing and let go of the pain.

Cast your circle and invite each Element in to help you in your magical work. Sit with each Element in turn speaking to them out loud or in your mind and asking for their qualities to enhance and assist in your work. I love this part! Then light a candle. You can also rub it with a healing oil of your choice beforehand (I like Tea Tree oil for healing). You can also write your name on a candle going down, if you wish for something to be released. I don't usually inscribe candles, but check with yourself whether it resonates. Something tells me it might work where numbers, specific words or conditions are involved.

Prepare your water, pour it into a bowl and put all the ingredients in slowly one by one. Do this with your hands over the bowl, as if charging (transmuting the energy from your hands into an object with intention). Start visualising your "wound" and each Element healing it in turn, sending light into it. Continue with this powerful visualisation for a while, imagining the healing light going into the wound and radiating through your whole body. When you feel you have charged the water fully and have truly experienced that healing in your body, drink the water and feel it going down your throat and into your body. Continue imagining your body and your wound being cleansed and purified and the healing light radiating through each cell in your body. It is a wonderful sensation and a powerful spell.

You will know when the spell is done. Sometime you will need to sit longer in your visualisation, other times less. Just follow your intuition and don't forget to breathe and when it is done, you simply complete by saying "This is done!" "So it will be!" or "Mote it be!"

Exercises

- Align with certain candles and oils if you are called to do so and would like to incorporate these elements into your magic practice.
- Examine the healing spell provided and produce your own variation, if you wish, to be used at the next Waning Moon. Be creative!

Intuitive Witch's tips

- When working with candles, on completion do not blow flames out, use a candle snuffer. Experiment with this and find out the sensory difference for yourself. You will understand intuitively what I mean when you practice yourself. It is a gentler way of "letting go" of the flame and completing your spell, without interrupting the flow of the spell. It is not as sudden or abrupt. Whatever you choose to do, please remember each spell does require a beginning with a clear intention and a proper ending. This will be confirmed to you by intuition and if it tells you

something else, be curious.
- While developing an intuitive practice take what resonates and leave the rest.

Chapter 13

Working Intuitively with Spells

All my work is built on the intuitive energy of my inner voice and what I do is simply listen to any vibrational changes within my emotional and physical bodies, which let me know when something needs to push through or there is a particular area that needs attention. Things can also present themselves to us in a physical reality; facts will be laid out in front of us challenging us to deal with whatever it is that is present.

As I said in the *Intuitive, Trust and Ethics* chapter when it comes to spell work, I would usually use it as a last resort or as part of the "whole package". For example, if I was to do a healing spell, I would first ensure that all the other healing techniques have been implemented, e.g. drinking water, eating well, getting fresh air, stretching, good sleep, or seeing a doctor, if necessary. I would do a spell to help with the facilitation of all the changes I wish to appear in my body when dealing with any pain, or just to assist in manifesting a change on a physical level (like bringing in more vitality in support of all the changes already in place). One can also apply this to a psychic "cleaning". The point that is important here is that spells are fantastic and very powerful tools to help you with whatever you are trying to manifest, but the process should not be one of "must do a spell" and ignore all other options. It is more of "what if I did this spell and that spell to support this thing and that thing", and should be undertaken after a period of self-healing and implementing things in your reality to manifest change.

Another thing to mention is that spell work should always be done when your energy is at its highest for a particular issue, when there is a knowing or even an urgency to invite magical workings into your process of manifesting, e.g. "money difficulties/illness that just won't go away". The best time is when the calling to do a spell is at its highest and the need is at its greatest. You WILL know when the time is right.

What NOT to do: proceed with the spell if the energy is low and here I am referring to your *own* energetic vibration, rather than a *need's* vibration.

If you don't feel well emotionally or physically, it would make sense not to push through even though it might be the Full Moon or any other traditional alignment. Leave it until next time. You should not rush with the work if there is no time either, wait till you have time to yourself to focus 100%. One might feel under pressure to perform a spell or a ritual (yes, it does happen), to coincide with certain festivals and Moon cycles, but, as I discovered over time, this goes against my intuition and I don't always feel aligned with the intention to do something if something inside of me says "not the right time". These are all external distractions or, perhaps, psychological automatic behaviours we are used to. Always listen to your inner voice, observe your body's signals and let your emotional body be free with what needs to come up and be communicated.

With spell crafting it is a good idea to look for things to raise your vibration before engaging in any practice. Remember spells don't only require focus but also an open-heart vibrating on the level of unconditional love. This is very important for the work you do to be effective. Remember never set an intention on hurting anyone or anything, it will simply come back to you twice as strong.

Love spells

Love spells are a good example of using your intuition while also being aware of the ethics and integrity within your work. A question often arises with regards to whether love spells are the right thing to do or if they are somehow wrong? Well, what do you think and feel about it? What is your reaction? It depends on your understanding of what a love spell is and of magic work in general. Refer back to all that you have learnt and reflected on before coming up with your own definition and the way love spells might be put together, if at all, in your own practice.

I think there is a difference between "putting a spell on someone" and doing a love spell. Do you see the difference?

Witchcraft practice is ethically bound (to me for sure) with a principle that you can do whatever you wish as long as you harm no one. Intuition will confirm that intention every time, in my experience. Enchanting someone without their knowledge is harming and goes against their free will. This doesn't correspond with any of the qualities of the Divine Feminine or the sacred practice of unconditional love and respect. You might disagree. Explore it for yourself.

What love spells are to me is a magical work of inviting more love into your life and into your heart, and directing it towards your family, surroundings or the world. It is a general increasing of the LOVE vibration around you and the act of you aligning with that energy to multiply the vibration of unconditional love. When you align with that vibration you will invite more of it into your life and it will be attracted to you in many ways. That's what love spells are to me.

They are gentle, soothing and light and not focused on setting a trap for someone without their knowing or agreement to being involved.

For love spells I use lots of crystals and flowers; tools my intuition often points towards.

I might also align with the Water element for these spells, as Water is the basis of our emotional qualities and very healing, just like love. You can be as creative with these as you want. You can use a pink candle for romantic connections, or a red one to invite more passion into your life and awaken that flame or a white one to connect with the spirit love. You can also write a rhyming spell for this particular intention or draw a beautiful picture. Be creative. Love, creativity, passion and imagination are a good mix.

Ending a spell

Okay, now we have performed all the spells and sent all our intentions into the Universe, what happens next? The best thing to do once a spell is done, is to forget about it.

By forgetting I mean try not to think about it or discuss it with anyone (not even in your own head). Simply go about your life as usual. Make sure when you do spells that they feel complete to you before you say "Mote it be!" or "It is done!" or whatever phrase is unique to your practice. You will feel whether a spell is complete or not. For me some spells are very quick-acting and others are not so. I might spend hours in a visualisation when working a spell, because I tap into something so soothing and beautiful that I enjoy the energy immensely. I make sure I savour every second and set my intention as strongly as possible during that time and align with it fully before I come out. You will know when it is time to bring your workings to a natural ending.

Exercise
- Think about what other spells you might want to try.

Chapter 14

Intuition and Working in Nature

Magic is deeply rooted in nature. Nature is the holder of the old ways and the wisdom of the Universe. It is the original divine source of spirit and life to me.

"Nature is a sacred cradle of sun's rays, butterflies' wings, tree leaves, rain drops and a nurturer of the essence and beauty of all souls..."
(Natalia Clarke, 2017)

If you work regularly in close collaboration with nature, your magic practice will grow stronger and your connection with yourself and the world will deepen over time.

What I like to do, first of all, when going to the woods is to sit against a tree, climb a tree, lie on the ground or simply walk barefoot (which can be done anywhere, not just in the woods). This is always my way of connecting with the Elements and spirit of nature through grounding into my body. I try to tune into the smells, textures, temperature and sounds around me to merge with the energy of a forest. You can experiment with it.

In my sacred place outside, there is a particular tree with a gentle vibration of the Mother. I always feel quite small in comparison to it yet we have similar vibration. I like to hug it and press my face against its warm bark and imagine this tree enveloping me in its arms and my body filling with white soothing light. Try it or find your own unique way to connect to trees.

My visits to the woods also come to me intuitively. I find that I will often "be called" into the woods when something needs clarifying, doing or is in need of understanding. This applies to magical workings too, such as spell crafting. There will usually be a specific thing that I am called to do. It is always because there is either a message I need to receive, or because I need to release something. Sometimes a calling comes from my body and most often I notice it feeling like "thirst" or a deep hunger for connection. It is a primal and instinctual feeling, very much felt in the body and clear in my awareness.

To follow on from the connection with nature and creating/performing magical workings in an outside space, I would like to share the Elements' spells with you, as well as a couple of spells created and performed in nature. You can easily incorporate these into your practice and/or create your own. They are all beautifully simple and very powerful. Sometimes in magic, I find, less is definitely more. I am a big fan of simplicity especially when working in nature. All you need is an open heart, clear intention and a wish to connect with nature in unconditional love.

Earth spell

From my experience Earth spells take time to manifest. Just like a seed that takes time to grow, they are slower but the results are lasting. When you plant something into the Earth, it takes its time to nurture and protect it, to look after it before letting it out into the world with the fruits of its labour.

One simple spell with Earth is to ask for something to manifest into the physical, e.g. you would like to grow your business or you would like more people to join your group or you would like to be able to meet more people or find more unique products or whatever it might be. You wish for something to materialise.

All you need is a candle and a rock, a stone or a crystal or any object you don't mind parting with; something that feels right.

Find a place outside to do this spell. Create a sacred circle, light your candle (colour of your choice here, I prefer white), call in all the Elements to help you with the main focus on the Earth, breathe, visualise your desire/need and set it into the object. Then lovingly bury it into the ground and let the candle burn out. Close the circle and it is done!

Remember always that if you are taking something from nature, please do it with gratitude and deep appreciation and ask for permission. I prefer to collect things from the ground and not touch the trees. For example, I wouldn't break branches off. You can also give something in return, but be mindful of nature and objects that might pollute the environment.

Water spell

Water spells can be either fast or slow working. They are healing, releasing and full of purifying qualities. You can perform these spells at either a quiet brook in the woods or the ocean, the sea, a fast river or a waterfall. Sometimes you might even be told the specific place you need to go to perform a certain water spell. It has happened to me before. When choosing a body of water you can match your need and intention to the flow and energy of the water place that you choose be it fast or slow flowing, rigorous or gentle.

These spells are great for letting go of negativity, releasing tension or asking for healing relationships. Please always work with releasing spells implementing love and gratitude for any experience even if it is a negative one. This can also be a "forgiveness" spell. Water can be balancing emotionally, and when your emotions need attention working with water is a very soothing and healing experience.

I would like to offer a feather spell for you here. Find a feather and choose a Water place to connect with. Visualise yourself releasing and being cleansed. It can be very powerful to become a body of water in your visualisation, to step into its power and vibration, shapeshift into what it might feel like to be in the flow. When you feel you are clear in your intention, kiss your feather gently and release it into the water. Either let it go downstream or just gently let it flow away on its own. Don't forget to breathe and enjoy the delicious magical connection with the Water element.

Fire spell

Fire spells are quick-working. They are transformative, driven, firm and purposeful. First and foremost, they banish. It is a sort of releasing, but in a very quick, firm and decisive manner.

One popular spell and one of my favourites, due to its simplicity and effectiveness, is a spell with a bay leaf. Light a candle, which is usually red, dark purple or black. You can align this spell to a particular Moon cycle (Full Moon is good).I sometimes use a white candle and change the energy a little to make the flow of the intention a bit smoother.

Light your candle, visualise a sacred circle around you and continue breathing deeply. Keep your goal firmly in your mind. Then take the bay leaf and write your intention in one word on the leaf, e.g. "fear" or "worries", etc. Use just one word to sum up what you are trying to do. Then while continuing to visualise whatever it is that you are releasing burn the leaf in the flame. It is done!

Air spell

The Air Element is fast yet gentle, neither here nor there, "now you see it and now you don't" type of energy. It is forever moving, transforming, coming and going. With Air I find one needs to align, which requires some practice, as it is neither staying still nor can be seen easily. It is illusive and mystical. Please note that this is my interpretation and you might feel completely differently about the Air element. Do explore and experiment for yourself.

When something is released with the Air element it is usually with a sense of asking for help, for connection or asking to form an alliance. I see Air spells as a release that goes further. When intentions are released into the Air, you don't know where they might end up; think about it carefully. Be sure you feel completely aligned with your intentions and with the Element when doing an Air spell. I would encourage you to sit with this one for a while and see what needs and desires come up, which you think might be best released with the Air. I have found these are good for releasing bad habits and yearnings of the heart.

What I do mostly with Air spells is I set up the usual circle, use candles and burn something written on a piece of paper (for example, a bad habit you wish to let go of) and then release ashes into the wind outside.

Holly Tree Releasing Spell

Working with trees in spellcasting is a deeply nourishing experience. I also find trees hold all the Elements, as a whole, which is incredibly potent when tuning into their energy. Because of trees' huge potential with regards to their energetic signature spells are often very simple when working with trees.

One morning (winter time) a familiar energy called me into the woods. I woke up feeling whole, balanced and knowing I would be doing some restorative magic. After having a heart-felt conversation with a friend the call of the forest increased and armed with a small white candle and my 'charged' palms (my hands buzz before doing a spell) I stepped on a path familiar on my way to the sacred grove.

At a distance as I approached, I very clearly saw the face of the Maiden (beautiful she was) outlined at the entrance to the woods, which then changed to the Crone's face. It made me smile and I bowed, as I always do, entering the forest.

I sat on a familiar holly tree and created a place for my energies to be sent into a simple white candle with dry leaves around it representing release. The holly tree spoke to me of unconditional love, resilience and protection. I invited all the Elements to assist me with this work. Fire to transform, Air to clarify, Earth to neutralise and Water to cleanse. It felt just right as I recalled the names of people who were in need of a release from the turmoil in their souls at that time. As I released the energy from my palms to all four directions I saw and heard the last remaining leaves falling off trees all around me and I saw a deer just a few meters away from me. We looked and acknowledged each other for a few minutes. I asked for peace in the world and a release of all that is no longer in service to us. It was a waning moon time and the right time to let things go.

As the candle was about to burn out, I picked up a couple of leaves surrounding the candle and burnt them in the flame. Once this was done, I collected it all together and buried it under the tree in the rich, most soil. It is one of my favourite spells, which can be adapted depending on what's needed. I always feel great afterwards.

I exited the grove and the woods with a bow and on my return, I engaged with the water Element by taking a shower to reinvigorate my energy.

Success/Business spell in nature

This example is a direct extract from my journal, which you can adapt as you like:

With my increasing Fire energy of productivity this month, I am drawn to doing a Success/Business spell. I feel that warm fire burning within me and a spell materialising within my awareness and I feel propelled into action. I sit down and create a spell using my intuition and collecting all the information that is flooding into me this morning and within minutes I know what to do and how. I select the wording I like, collect and prepare all the tools and decide to go out to do this spell work in the woods. You can certainly do it at home too, in your sacred space, whatever you are drawn to in the moment. I always encourage going with whatever is present for you.

As I walk towards the woods, I feel incredibly excited, buzzing with the electric energy of the Sun, which is shining bright this morning. It is chilly, but I like the cold very much. It invigorates all of my senses; I feel alive and ready for action. I walk fast and smile all the way to the place that I intuitively knew I was going to do this spell this morning. It is a different place from my usual one. I feel, or rather intuitively know, that switching places for my magic work sometimes can create new energies and allows for the flow of energy to move more freely as it is not always confined to one place. I also had a sense of a 'big hug', an embrace of the whole archetype of the woods, which expanded my sense of belonging. I wanted to include all of it within me. I bow, as I walk into the grove.

I am intuitively drawn to a tree root, which is perfect for this type of spell, as not only have trees been my most vital sources of guidance and support, but their roots are super important to me, as they are touching Gaia and her energy is flowing through these magnificent forest giants. It is that energy I want to tap into.

I create a mini circle and here is the spell in action: materials you use, the order you do things in, chanting, etc.

- *Yarrow for luck and Bay Leaf for protection and stability.*
- *A bee is a spirit animal of success and abundance and also aligns with hard work, perseverance and endurance.*
- *It is a Fire and Earth spell based mainly on the male energies, which are around this time of the year.*

I set up a circle in my usual way with crystals in each direction (sometimes I take my set up with me outside). I called upon all Elements to assist me. Placed a bee wax candle in a small glass bowl filled with crushed herbs and positioned it in the middle. Underneath I placed my business card. Visualising success I lit the candle (I used a small one) and sat with the intention of bringing the energy of success into my business.

I am filled with this incredible joy of yet again having connected with the magic of the forest, Earth and nature. I put my arms around a tree and instantly images of luxurious nature come to me. I also had an idea of a new magic book I need to produce come to me in that moment. This is so beautiful in a felt sense that I am bursting with joy. As I walk out of the woods, I really do feel like I did some serious work and I bathe my face in the winter Sun standing still for a while before bowing to the grove saying "I love you so much!"

On my return home I drink a blend of tea, which is 'feminine' in nature. Intuitively again and this is very important to me in my magic work, I am drawn to balancing the energies. As most of the work this morning had male energy origins and the qualities I had to invoke were of Fire predominantly, I feel I need to balance them out with my feminine energy and I drink this tea, which is delicious .I have a deep sense of belonging, comfort and home. You can make your own blend of herbs to empower your feminine flow daily.

Exercises

- Have a go at creating variations of spells offered using your intuition.
- Notice if you are drawn to feminine or masculine energy more in your practice? Is there a pattern? Do the Elements correspond as suggested for you or are they different when working with spells?
- Go on discovering what herbal teas you like and how they make you feel?

Chapter 15

Intuition, Divine Feminine and Sacred Self-care

Example from my journal:

A vibe of steady pace manifested on this beautiful and gentle Beltain morning. The air was still and fresh and very present through my body. Something landed in me this morning. How interesting the timing, so divine. I felt something has arrived finally to say 'this is it', 'the time is now'. It was like a door opened into the light of green and as I dug my hands into fresh soil, I felt my heart softening and breathing and becoming steady.

In our society and throughout the centuries it has, for women, been all about 'go, go, go' and 'do, do, do' the more tasks the better, the more organised and achieved the more valuable you will be perceived as. Such a false race for time, more jobs and tasks, more activities, etc. No wonder maidens coming out of attachment are exhausted and feeling low in self-worth. Remember ignoring intuition and lacking in self-care is self-abandonment pure and simple.

This morning the Triple Goddess stood strong in her message. Being free and spacious is vital for manifestation of the whole within a being. Slower is not lazy, slower is wiser. It is intuitive, flowing, knowing. Rest and reflection are necessary for manifesting true identity and purpose. I felt it slot into my body this morning like a piece that's not always acknowledged or allowed. I have been aware of my self-created freedom for some years now and have been consciously practicing my gratitude for all that it represents, for all that it's given me. The most sacred thing, which I have always wanted.

Freedom is so desirable and often seen as an unachievable dream. When it arrives, we resist it, putting ourselves in prison, overloading ourselves with more to do to contradict it, as it is not something we are used to. A sadness hovers over it within, as we know we truly desire to be free, but can't allow it.

It takes a lot of practice to feel completely free and present in a slow pace of life. It is the most precious gift, which, it seems, we all seek. Now is the time to say YES to it and recognise freedom as truly ours for the taking.

When beginning to work with your sacred feminine I encourage you to start by reflecting on the following qualities within yourself: nurturing, wisdom, life, creation, birth, healing, receptivity, intuition, insight, compassion, warmth, creativity, growth, reconstruction, the Moon, connecting, receiving.

Your work as a magician will grow stronger, as you allow yourself to stay as centred as possible and get in touch with the qualities of the sacred feminine within you. It is about connecting with the Goddess in you, your feminine and sacred power. The untamed, pure, wild, raw potential you came into this reality to explore and embody.

To come in contact with your inner Goddess is to explore and connect with the qualities of the Divine Feminine and allow these energies to come to life and express themselves through you.

These qualities have often been either suppressed in women in order to survive and fit in, or oppressed to the point of fear and rejection of the sacred, wild energy that is within us. In this world we as women often give to the point of depletion and complete self-abandonment. We "hold things together", hence controlling our emotions; not living from the heart, but from a point of, (now becoming outdated, yet deeply rooted), patriarchal reference of what "female" should and shouldn't be. All of these are distortions of what is truly ours, untamed, free-flowing, and deeply intuitive. We now look not to conform, but to rediscover what we really are.

To me, sacred feminine has three faces and the energies come as the Maiden, the Mother and the Crone (more on this later on in the book). They correspond to the cycles of life and death, which are represented in nature's seasons. When something dies, something is born again. The wheel of nature constantly turns and changes. Each of those aspects of the Goddess carry unique qualities of the whole of the sacred feminine and it is within each of us that the Goddess must awaken and breathe magic into our lives and senses once again.

Magical housework

We begin with clearing a space for the energies of the Goddess to be able to come in fully and express herself through your consciousness. The following tools and techniques are designed to consciously raise your vibration and when your vibration is high, wisdom comes in easier. You are more receptive to the flow of all things magical.

Consider the following practice. When you wake up in the morning, be intent on doing the following and observe how each step makes you feel. Be 100% WITH yourself in everything you do. Practice mindfulness as you go about these tasks. Write your experiences down at the end of the day in your journal.

- Open windows in your house to allow the energy to cleanse and begin to move.
- Do some stretching exercises or Yoga, if you already have a practice. If you don't, consider taking up some physical practice in the morning. It can be anything. For me it is walking and stretching with trees.
- Light a candle, whatever colour comes to you on that morning. Be intuitive, curious and open to what comes to you. If nothing comes, a white candle is always a good choice.
- Light some incense. Choose a fragrance you like or are drawn to on that morning. I often go with sage,

frankincense or apple.

- Sage your room or the whole house to cleanse any negative unwanted influences and stagnated energy.
- Drink water and visualise your body becoming awake and cleansed by the water, as you take it in.
- Wash your face with full awareness, like cleaning a mirror ready to reflect and be reflected upon.
- Meditate/visualise on all the things that you find beautiful and fulfilling in your life. Focus on increasing joy and pleasure in your reality.
- Put some music on and dance or you might want to lie down and visualise to music, if you feel like something less energetic in that moment. You choose what you are drawn to.
- Go out and buy yourself some flowers or collect some from your garden. It can also be twigs or herbs, anything that calls to you. Notice colours you are drawn to. Is there a particular fragrance or texture? How do you feel?

Sacred self-care

What do I mean by sacred self-care? This links in with self-awareness, which can grow through listening to yourself with complete trust and seeing powerful results in your way of being with yourself and the world. It means giving yourself what your inner voice asks of you or points you towards; giving yourself what you need in the moment by listening to your intuition; treating yourself with compassion, love and respect, as you would any divine energy. It is looking after yourself on all levels: physical, mental, emotional and spiritual. Give your body the best food and exercise. Learn to trust your body when you feel something is unsafe using intuition also means looking after the physical aspect of yourself. Provide your mind with empowering intellectual stimulus and conversations that make you happy, contained and productive. On an emotional level self-care means meeting your needs and always honouring your feelings.

If a child cries you attend to it; why wouldn't you do that for yourself? See everything you feel and experience as valid and worthy of your attention.

Self-care in a spiritual sense looks like creating a unique and nourishing spiritual practice, be it sitting in ritual, being creative with your craft, nature communion, journaling, etc.

If one aspect of your whole self-care falls short the others are not as effective. Self-care is paramount for magic practice as a spiritual discipline.

A jar of qualities

Here is another fun project I would like to share with you, which is a great way to consolidate what you have learnt so far when getting in touch with your inner Goddess.

This exercise is called *A Jar of Qualities*. Decide what resonates with you and also how far you wish to take this. It is a great integration tool in getting to know yourself and becoming aware of any blockages, rejections or denials of your own "goodness" or being ambivalent about your own "badness". This will aid you in your magic practice.

Remember, the Goddess exists in both light and dark, life and death and it is important to embrace your whole being as one divine energy.

1. Find an empty jar. Choose it intuitively by size, shape, texture and feel.
2. You might want to decorate it how you like; you might want to put lights into it, paint it on outside, put flowers in it or keep it simple.
3. Spend some time with your jar, may be find a specific place to keep it in.
4. On a piece of paper write ONE quality you identify and

know in yourself. Choose one quality a day. If that is too hard do it over a week or a month. Choose your own paper type, colour, and texture. You might wish to use other materials, like cloth, velvet or even tree bark. This exercise is yours to experiment with.

5. Once you have written down a quality, set an intention to spend some time with that quality in quiet contemplation and really feel it within yourself. You might want to use a mirror while getting in touch with the chosen quality. Then find ways of manifesting it in your daily life, for example if you choose "kind" do something kind for someone or yourself. This is a simple example and I would encourage you to go deep within and excavate as many qualities as you can. Be specific and tune into the nuances of your divine essence.

6. Note that you might want to choose what one might call "negative" qualities too and spend time with those, looking at and integrating them into your whole self. You might find that what was once perceived or believed to be negative transforms or grows into a positive aspect of your being.

7. Always look at any negatives, as your strengths, with compassion, as almost all perceived distortions are our wounded parts wanting love. Can you see how all qualities can serve you as long as you are honest about the process and the energies around those qualities are not distorted? For example, you are not denying something that is within you and you are able to take your projections back and integrate them. Try to be completely aware of what arises within you, when, and why.

8. Do one quality every day (or whatever frequency you might choose) and fill up your magic jar as slowly or as quickly as you wish, but ensure you really spend needed amount of time with each of your qualities.

9. Enjoy the process. It is beautifully empowering and freeing.

Ideas flowed in this morning as I began my day. My intention was to make a set up for my work, first of all, in order to facilitate energetic, mindful and psychic work to come. Such a place would normally be my altar.

As the theme unfolding in my awareness was to do with the body, I wanted to include the four Elements. As the Earth/nature holds them so do we in our bodies. Incense for Air, a bowl for Water, wood for Earth, candles for Fire and purple crystal for Spirit. We are one and my intention was to include nature into the work as I usually do. This allows for deeper insight and connection to myself and to the outside world. It is stormy weather outside today, so I had to bring the Elements in, which was very relevant in terms of exploring them within myself.

The idea was to explore a particular habit/attachment of mine to do with food and look into whether there was an emotional signature that was stuck within my physical container. I did this with my other physical habit with great success previously. The aim is to discover what need or emotion might lie beneath a certain behaviour. It helped enormously and really is the best way to work with any addictive or habitual behaviour, which potentially harms us. It is about bringing the wound up to the light to heal it consciously and then meeting the need that we are unconsciously trying to meet by turning to various activities and things.

This morning didn't go according to plan and I do love it when that happens. First of all, I noticed huge resistance to doing this work and I realised I was delaying. Once I was ready for my journeying, I was pulled out of it pretty much straight away and insights came in strong and fast before I even did anything. I found that quite striking as it was quick and very illuminating.

I was told loud and clear before I started doing the body scan that it is my broken tooth that needed attention and 'haven't I procrastinated enough about it?' and why wouldn't I attend to my teeth when there is such a clear need. I felt well and truly told off! And yes, why wouldn't I? Is that a loving thing to do? To ignore areas that need fixing in my body? I booked my appointment immediately. The Universe had an opening for me in the next half hour (what are the chances).

So, the insight here is to attend to the things that we are actually conscious of first and foremost before delving deeper into possible unconscious reasons for whatever it is that is causing us discomfort in the physical. Quite simple, right? But how many of us are ignoring what is clearly visible, felt and screaming for help? Lack of self-compassion, acknowledgement and self-love could potentially be dangerous not just to our bodies but our well-being as a whole. It felt very different for me at that time as again there was such avoidance and resistance to making that phone call regardless of how loud the inner voice was. I hesitated as I realised that it was not familiar for me to stand up for myself, so to speak, and I wondered how often I had previously ignored this need. Earlier last year I would have been in real trouble by ignoring something very serious if it wasn't for someone else pushing me to make the call. I know I would not have done it myself and I am scared to think what could have been if I ignored the signs.

So, my advice is to deal with what is manifesting, felt and present in the moment. What you are fully aware of right now in your body? Where is the pain, imbalance or discomfort? Attend to that. Deal with that as soon as you can because why wouldn't you? Why would your body be less important in wanting to be well than anyone else's? We are used to taking care of others, as it is looked upon as a positive and valued thing to do in society. Self-sacrifice is an act that we are told will somehow lift you up above and merge you with God. But what about you? Aren't you as one with God and nature already? If we really think about it, it doesn't make sense. It is time to shift our thinking to centre around self-love, compassion, and listening to our bodies as a step on the path towards well-being as a whole, complete person.

Ritual cleansing bath

Once you have cleared the space for the energies of the Divine Feminine to flow freely in your physical space, we can start to look on the inside with the intention of clearing our emotional and sensory bodies, so that the inner light of the Goddess begins to shine brighter.

The Goddess comes with fresh, vibrant, fragrant, bright energy and fills our awareness with new possibilities. She opens up new horizons. She is beautiful, sensual, soft and gentle.

Now I invite you to perform a Water ritual, spell, meditation – whatever you wish to call it. It is a beautiful sacred practice to bring you into alignment with the energy of the Goddess, to ask her for guidance and to cleanse your energy field so the essence within you will be able to shine brighter each day as you continue this journey. Very powerful!

Water is a well-known symbol of healing and purification. Immersing yourself in water has always been recognised in spiritual circles as a sacred act of cleansing oneself of anything that no longer serves you and that blocks your forward movement and growth. This ritual bath is not for physical washing, but for meditation and to affect changes in your reality.

For the spell you will need:

- Bath
- Rosemary and sage leaves (dry or fresh). If you don't have it, please do not worry, choose herbs that you like. You can also use essential oils instead, whatever your inner voice settles on
- White candles as many as you wish or can find
- Sea or Epsom salt

- A mirror (your bathroom mirror would be fine)
- Oil (a good one to use would be Sandalwood), but if not in possession, please use olive oil or one of your own choice

Pick a time when you will not be disturbed. Have all your items together. Run a bath with warm water and while it is running add herbs and salt to it. Light your candles and turn off any electric light.

Relax and release through breathing before going into the water. Set your intention and ask the Goddess, to hold your hand and guide you. Say the following:

Oh Divine Goddess cleanse me now of all that holds me back and stops my growth. BE my guiding force. Hold me while I embrace my fullest potential, lay open my heart to growth

Immerse yourself into the water with your face and hair, so that every part gets wet. Lay back and get comfortable.

Appreciate how you feel, reflect on what you might be holding on to, what you are grateful for. Think about relationships, jobs, family, money or anything else that comes to you while you reflect on the whole of your experience in that moment. Be aware of any anxieties, fears, and blockages coming up in you, any memories or traumas. Let it wash through you. Whatever comes allow it to show itself and review all the pain that you have ever had and anything that ever held you back either externally or internally. As you think and review each aspect, make an affirmation to your Goddess-self and the Universe as a whole:

I release this, it leaves me now

Stay in meditation for a few minutes releasing your thoughts and becoming an observer of your experience. Focus on your breathing and allow the energy to flow through you without being distracted by interference of the mind. You can continue with the ritual bath for as long as you wish.

When you are done, get out of the bath and standing in front of the mirror without drying yourself off think of all the things that you have released. And affirm:

All that I have released I now leave behind me

What has been released remains in the water and with the opening of the draining hole will return to the Mother Earth for regeneration.

You continue the spell by looking at your face in the mirror. Be aware of how you feel, of your inner voice, of your attitude towards yourself. This is important to notice and after you take a deep breath, say to yourself:

I love thee with everything that I am. I am a child of the Goddess, who she loves.

This spell/ritual can be performed at any time and as often as you wish and the effects will strengthen as you practice more.

Body wisdom

As you develop your practice and deepen your relationship with yourself as a result I would invite you to be present with your physical body whether you do some walking, stretching, running, yoga, dancing or any other exercise, which involves your participation with the Earth's reality and energy in whatever way works for your unique body.

Our female bodies hold a lot of wisdom. Just imagine the knowledge contained in our bodies' cells through generations. Bodies hold all our emotions, scars, wounds and traumas. The body remembers everything that has ever happened to you. Our mind often seeks to banish anything unpleasant or traumatic into the unconscious and it can feel like we forget and some material is no longer accessible, but the body always remembers. Developing respect and reverence for our bodies is a crucial part on your journey to developing a deeply meaningful magical practice. Without the body it will not be possible.

Eat clean, drink green

To experience the lightness and a higher vibration within our physical body we need to eat and drink clean. What we give to the physical will manifest in the light and vibrancy of your emotions and spiritual connection within your own Divinity.

The Goddess within us is beautiful and vibrant. She is attuned to the energies of the Universe and her cells are always open to receiving messages and guidance. This is the state that we can all manifest through clearing out the body and listening to the message our body is sending us. Start your own clean eating and drinking practice:

- Drink a glass of water (pure or flavoured, as per suggestions or create your own) on the hour every hour for two days. Incorporate this practice into your life. Prepare yourself for amazing results!

Some suggestions for water are: lemon, cucumber and strawberry or lemon, basil and strawberry. Begin to introduce a clean, organic (where possible), vegan (if you prefer), fresh light food into your day for at least one meal, e.g. a vibrant, organic, fresh salad or two meals, e.g. a smoothie/green juice in the morning and a salad at lunch.

Go with what you are drawn to and enjoy it. As always be aware of how you feel and what is happening within you and outside of you, be open, mindful and very present with everything that you do.

As one exercise to get in touch with your body I would invite you to experience *Mindful Barefoot Walking*. If you can't do it outside, do it in your home on the floor. If walking is difficult simply take off your shoes and place your feet on the ground/floor/grass in the garden. The aim is to be 100% present with the energy of the Goddess and her strong supportive energy, which are holding you safe, grounded and balanced. Now set in your goals and aspirations in life.

Another way is to meditate quietly for five minutes to get in touch with your physical vibration every morning. How do you feel? Energetic or quiet? Do you prefer to move fast or slow today? Attune to the energy within your physical body, which will also give you clues to your emotional state on any given day. According to your energetic vibration, choose a physical activity to tune into the Earth element of the Goddess and seek to express her energy through your body.

Once you have mindfully experienced your connection to the Earth through using your body, I would like you to do a meditation to go even deeper into connection with the very essence of your physical body. This meditation is often surprising for many and shows how many of us are out of touch with our bodies; taking this sacred vessel of our soul for granted or simply not noticing the work it does for us on a daily basis. It is incredible how we all sometimes forget and disconnect from what is our foundation, but the Goddess draws us back into it, to our fundamental structure, to our roots within.

Meditation

First get comfortable and settle into a gentle breathing rhythm. Let go of the worries and concerns that your mind is holding. Take your time and once that is done begin to breathe into your heart centre. Connect with your heart before going down to your feet and begin building your skeleton. This meditation is about getting in touch with your structure, with your bones. Visualise each bone in your body in whatever way you wish to do that and get a sense of what it feels like, looks like and even what it might say to you?

Really feel your bones and in your world of creative imagination build a skeleton of yourself, your support system. Notice how you feel about your body once you finish the exercise.

Draw a picture of your skeleton and observe any possible weak spots that you can identify, as well as points that stand out. Did you feel or see any imbalances or anything else that came up for you? Try and represent it visually on a piece of paper. It is a powerful exercise. Note all the insights that you get from it and write it down in your journal.

Qualities and projections

I would like to invite you to do a bit of psychological evaluation and awareness exercises on yourself using the following questions:

- What do you like about being a woman and why?
- What don't you like about being a woman and why?

It might help if you look at people that you know, women that you know or have known throughout your life and see if you can pinpoint anything that you loved or disliked about them. Then, look within and see if you can identify those traits in yourself. If you can identify your projections - great, go with gentle observation, no judgement, punishment or rejection. Try to embrace everything that comes up with unconditional respect and empathy. This is important for a successful integration of the whole! Remember that even the Goddess possesses various degrees of "good" and "bad" and that is a natural order in all things. Nature is innately dark and light.

Note down in your journal what you come up with, and ask any questions you might have. As you go about your day, also see if any synchronicities (meaningful coincidences in your reality) come up for you. Those carry messages that wish to attract your attention and as you put the questions out into the Universe, the Goddess will guide you. Enjoy the process!

Synchronicities

What is a synchronicity? It is an event or a particular occurrence in your life, which seems to have no explanation yet in time a meaning is born out of it, which makes sense to you. It can often go unnoticed at the time, but with practice you can learn to observe synchronicities intentionally. You might even start keeping a synchronicities journal or add your observations to the journal you already have.

When working with spells, which is setting an intention and inviting a particular energy to facilitate a change, synchronicities often will start popping up in your reality. They are like sign posts towards opportunities, a magical "set-up" of events, experiences and coincidences to bring a goal to a particular manifestation. If you listen to yourself fully and follow the signs, you can be sure things will happen. Do not fear the process, trust yourself with everything that you do, see, feel and experience.

Can you think of any synchronicities that you are aware have happened in your life?

Exercise

- We have already looked at a lot of different exercises and practices, so, perhaps, you might simply take the time to absorb what's been talked about, reflect on your feelings and thoughts and experiment with it.

Chapter 16

Intuition and The Triple Goddess Aspects

What I refer to as the Triple Goddess are those three aspects of her, as the Maiden, the Mother, and the Crone. These three aspects of one Goddess carry different energies and are present within us all. Each manifests within and without not only at certain times of the year, but also in any given moment in our daily reality. It is a valuable tool to recognise energies as they arise and operate. For example, the Maiden vibration is the strongest during spring time when she awakes from the winter sleep and is born again followed by a marriage and then a childbirth. It can also be present when we feel "young" or adolescent depending on what we are faced with in our lives or what we are doing. It can be positive or negative, can feel sulky or moody or can manifest as carefree.

The Mother archetype is the summer energy, ripe and nurturing like Earth at harvest time and can also come about when you are around children and family life. The Crone is mostly present during the darker part of the year from October onwards and throughout winter. You might feel her energy when you act and behave with a certain wisdom or at a slower pace. She is non-reactive, but considerate, full of mystery and lessons.

I would like you to explore how true this is for you! Which aspects do you recognise within yourself and which ones do you resonate with the most? There is wisdom in knowing different parts of yourself and how you manifest the Goddess energies in your daily life.

My suggested exercise as part of your exploration is to, first of all, to go into nature (experiment with all four seasons). Immerse yourself in the Elements of the Goddess (Water, Fire, Earth and Air), experience each element in whatever way you find resonates with you. You might want to light a candle and burn a few twigs or you might want to have a bonfire. You might want to walk in Water barefoot or across the forest floor or stand somewhere high up and feel the wind on your face. These are all great ways to connect with what is divine within you and what is a natural flow of the Goddess, through the Elements and nature.

I also suggest a meditation to aid you in your exploration of the Triple aspect of the Goddess:

Triple Goddess Meditation

Begin, as always, by getting comfortable. Relax, pay attention to your breathing and let go of any worries and concerns that you are holding onto. Get in touch with your body. Once you are completely relaxed imagine yourself in a peaceful spot in nature. It can be any landscape that calls to you whether it is a seashore, a mountain range, a forest or a lake. Stay still and listen. What do you see and hear? What comes to your first? Is it the Maiden, the Mother or the Crone? Or do ALL three come to you at once? What does she do when encountering you? What does she say? Spend time with whatever aspect presents itself and stay in the meditation until you feel your exploration is complete. You may want to spend some time using the grounding techniques we have previously discussed when you come out of meditation.

Once you have had a chance to explore the Goddess aspects within yourself you might want to implement what you have learnt and explore your knowledge of the energies further in your life to get to know their archetypal manifestations. Focusing on the Maiden energies you might want to go and have some fun with your friends: do something joyous and carefree like dancing or playing games. You can also do it by yourself. With the Mother aspect you can spend time with children and looking after a home. What kind of mother are you? What is important to you? What touches your heart? This Mother aspect also applies to caring for older people. Older people contain both a child and a wise person within them. I find them fascinating and interesting and I always learn a lot when spending time around old people. With the Crone, is there anyone that you know you instantly think of when you think of the Crone? Go to them! Spend some time and listen to their stories. See how you feel.

Here is an experience I would like to share with you when I worked with the Triple Goddess aspect in ritual and visualisation, which provided me with the nourishing and rebuilding energy I needed.

Once I felt in need of reminding myself of the magic that ran through my veins. I was called to look deep within to revive my own potential, strength and power. I also needed to release the tension, doubt, anxiety and sadness that had accumulated within. I needed to engage with nature to obtain some restorative medicine and wisdom.

I have been called a lot lately to be present for others, to take care of the external things and people, which has left me starved for inner peace, reflection and care- taking of my own soul. I was in need of a ritual, of tears, focus and of attending to my soul's needs.

That morning I felt like hibernating, wrapping myself up warm and cosy in a luxurious thick blanket, covering my head with a purple scarf and snuggling up with a coffee in front of my altar. This felt so needed and timely. I was looking after myself in a way I hadn't been able to lately. Solitude was something I craved. I often reach that point when there is no path to take or choice to make other than sit in complete silence with myself, rocking myself into comfort and steering back to the road where I can get in touch with spirit.

I put on some music and began my journey in front of my altar with all the aspects of the Goddess present.

The Maiden: *wearing a thin white tunic, barefoot with her long hair dropping loosely on her shoulders she walks very softly upon the shore of a lake.*

I recognise the place. She moves her hands in a gentle dance and flowers drop from her fingers. She raises her arms in the air and flowers shoot out from under the ground opening up towards the new. There is an innocence, purity, beauty and translucency of spirit that surrounds her. She is the Element of water and air. She begins to fly over the lake continuing to scatter flowers on the water. I cry and cry. It is a beautiful sight and a powerful release for me. I missed her.

The Mother: *she is walking in a pine forest where trees reach high up into the sky. She looks up and around her. She wears a green dress and boots. There is light and confidence about her. She has earthly energy, a very pentacle type energy of manifestation and being firmly in the world. She walks along the pine forest tidying things up here and there, picking up branches and touching trees. She arrives at a point where a view opens up in front of her. I recognise this place. The sun is bright and warming and she smiles. There is a beautiful lake down below and forest stretches as far as the eye can see. She takes a deep breath and sits down on a tree stump. Animals gather around her legs; badgers and squirrels, and an owl lands on her lap. She strokes her very soft feathery body and all is content in the world and so am I.*

The Crone: *she is sitting on a rock looking out to the sea. I recognise these rocks. Wearing a long white cloak, which matches her white hair, she holds her walking wand firmly as a strong support for her frail body. She is knowing, content and at peace.*

There is nothing that she hadn't seen or done before. She is older than anything or anyone in this Universe.

She walks towards a pool of water coming off the rocks and whispers her spells and chants into the water taking out herbs from her pockets and throwing them in. She is forever magical and working for the good of the Earth. Then she walks into a cave and sits down with black crows surrounding her. Her inner comfort and peace are electric and striking. She begins to pull fire from under the earth with an upwards motion of her hands. With ease she brings it into reality and the air fills with warmth. She sits in deep reflection watching the flames, humming to herself. My heart opens up and I feel warm and comforted.

Exercises

- Explore if any of the three aspects is particularly difficult for you?
- Which aspect you are most drawn to?
- What is your interpretation of the three aspects?

Chapter 17

Casting Spells with Intuitive Drawings

Spells using drawings are great for your self-discovery and self-awareness work. Working in this way will facilitate your growth and understanding of your emotions and how you function. These are also effective for healing.

Let's imagine that one morning you woke up feeling angry and you didn't know why. Try just being with it for a minute or two and let it go through you without putting any pressure on it to go away, resisting it or trying to ignore or reject it. If you find yourself in a position to explore it further, I would suggest you go into a deeper visualisation of your emotional body. Go into deep breathing, ground and try to connect with that emotion that you are feeling. Where is it? What colour does it have? Let any images, colours, sounds, smells or symbols come to you spontaneously. Do not rush, force or overthink; allow the message to unfold completely.

When you are done, gently come back into your body and draw a picture of your experience. Do it straight away while the experience and feelings are still fresh in you. Begin to draw intuitively and spontaneously without engaging your mind. Allow the free flow of your creativity to direct you. Name the picture, explore it, and see how it feels and what it might be saying when you are done.

Once you have a drawing and you know what it says ask yourself what you need. Allow time for the answer to come into your awareness. What you do next is build your spell around that need, around that goal of what needs to happen for you to move forward. These spells are powerfully healing and transformative, as they come up directly from within you, from your unconscious precious material with intuition at the centre of them. You can use all the other tools and techniques (such as casting a circle, inviting in the Elements, using candles, crystals, etc.) that you wish to include. Choose them intuitively with the goal of facilitating and maximising the spell's effect.

Spells with drawings can also be good as a foundation for a release or a manifestation of whatever you are in need of.

Using spontaneous drawings in your spells is a very powerful way of accessing material that would otherwise be unseen and unknown/unconscious. It can reveal so much about you and the way you see things, your desires and needs, and about current obstacles and dislikes. It is good for breaking states of "stuckness" or confusion, for example. An interpretation is not always needed, as just drawing something out literally can help with feeling lighter and happier. It is one of my favourite ways to work and it is always wonderful to see shifts happen and insights come out of my drawings.

As an example, I did a Fire Element spell where I used this technique to release what was no longer needed (example below). I did the spell using a list of things I wanted to be released and I also did a drawing in a spontaneous way. I went with the flow without engaging my thinking mind, just letting my hand express on paper what was within me having set an intention to release all that needed to go.

An interesting observation was that when I wrote a list of things I wanted to release I was surprised that there didn't seem to be that many. Words didn't come easily, and I had to think about what to write. When using a drawing, however, there was a strong difference. It was so rich in colours and imagery that it filled the whole space. It shows that when your thinking is engaged it can block the emotional flow of the body, and all the important energetic stuff connected to feelings and memories, which are stored in the body. When drawing spontaneously all that material that needs to come out flows freely and in contrast to writing a list one can see just how much is inside and just how much needed to be released. If one stopped at just a list, the job would only be half-done. I hope this explains the power and value of incorporating this technique in your magical workings.

Here are some suggestions on how to go about using drawing in your spell-casting:

Find a quiet place where you won't be disturbed and just go for it. Draw whatever comes to you. You can use any materials for this, which you can choose intuitively. You might prefer doing a visualisation first before drawing. I go with spontaneous creating most of the time, i.e. putting pencil to paper without preparation or engaging with any thinking process. It is a process, which draws unconscious material out of darkness and into the light. It allows you to see what needs seeing in that moment.

Continue to tune into your body, as you go along and become aware of any feelings. Listen to where and what is appearing in your body. Most importantly let your creative material flow and trust that whatever is meant to come up will come up. You can think of an intention you become aware of while drawing and can let the Universe know what your intention is.

Fire spell example

Using the technique above I sat down to draw spontaneously. The Moon was waning, which was the perfect time to work on releasing things. I allowed my creativity to take over and relaxed into the awareness of my body, feelings and what I felt needed to be let go of at that moment. I used bright colours; reds, oranges and yellow. It felt warm and passionate. Once I was done, I decided to burn the drawing in my cauldron (be careful when using fire indoors; consider doing this outside). I used a violet candle with lavender oil to assist me in manifesting the energies I needed for the spell. Before burning it I placed my drawing underneath the lit candle and reflected on my feelings, goals, needs and desires and set my intention. Then I lit my candle and placed it in the cauldron. I rolled up my drawing and lit it slowly. I chanted watching it burn and disappear:

Let what no longer serves me
Fly away Fly away
Release me, Heal me, Cleanse me

Exercise

- Try out a spell with a drawing. Use the two techniques: either a visualisation before drawing, i.e. recording materials that came to you in your vision or drawing spontaneously. Notice which one you prefer, if there is a preference.

Chapter 18:

Intuitive Writing as a Spiritual Practice

A rhyming spell

I hardly ever write rhyming spells, however, many do and there could be good reasons for it depending on what is required or feels right in the moment. You might want to explore this for yourself to see where it leads you. The rhyming element sort of "seals the deal" and makes it tidy and neat. It also increases the vibration and intensifies your energy around your goal. This is my understanding, but it is not the only way.

The way I prefer doing this is again intuitively. If it comes to me, great, if it doesn't, I don't force it. It should all come to you if there is a specific need. Surrender to all possibilities.

I would suggest that you spend some time with an idea for a spell and in your meditative state allow for words and images to come through. If you think of a need, e.g. JOY or HEALTH what colours come to mind? What words are you aware of? Are there any images? Really listen to your senses. Then if you do come up with something use those words to make a message/ spell out of them whether rhyming or not. It can be as little as two rhyming lines or as long as you want depending on what you receive. You never know, you might be a natural receiver of words and a gifted constructor of rhymed spells! It is unique and individual just like everything in this practice. Give it a go! Here is an example of a rhyming healing spell:

Magic heals and candle burns,
Illness gone and health returns!

Repeat several times as you visualise illness leaving your body and health and vitality being restored. It is simple yet effective and powerful. I have used this one on many occasions.

Intuition is invaluable when partaking in writing. Something I became aware of more as I wrote more. It often feels similar to magic when you simply know what tools to use, how and when and the results just come together. It is the same with words, which come when one is tuned into emotions in the moment. It works when there is no overthinking and spontaneous leaps are taken in narratives. For sure, you edit and then edit some more, as you progress, but in my experience, that initial expression is often the most powerful. Poetry is one genre that often comes intuitively. Some words seem to come from nowhere and that is so exciting to me when writing.

Just like I would intuitively know what oil to use with what candle and what Goddess/God/deity would best support my work at a particular time, I would hear words coming out of me, which happen to be just right for what I am writing about.

My tip is not to think, but to feel and listen and follow with free writing. I also recommend free associations as often as possible with images, nature scenes, trees or seasons. Allow for whatever is called to come through. I think it stimulates and trains your imagination. It feels like magic and your intuition is your magic, your inner knowing that offers what is needed when it is needed.

This practice unfolded for me over the years revealing such gems from within my unconscious, which very often would align with what was needed generally in the world at any given moment. What a gift our intuition truly is. It takes us to places that are wonderful and magic, which then lead to magical experiences and connections. Nowadays there is no other way for me to write, but from the soul, spontaneously uttering the words, which are ready to be spoken.

I also always find that later on at some point, someone comes along, who clearly needs to hear that message I blogged or shared about at one point or another I can then go to that piece and share it with the person in need passing on my experience whether it is an exercise, a spell, a psychological healing technique or an exploration. It can also be images. Most people can access beautiful images of nature and landscapes easily. Combined with intuitive writing pieces it is a feast for the eyes, ears and heart.

It feels wonderful to be able to express myself, most of the time spontaneously, as these things come up in me at random moments. Sometimes it is one blog post a month, other times it is up to five blogs a day. I go with whatever is presenting itself, as I consider it important to express whatever knocks on the door of my awareness. This practice can be applied to journal writing, novel or story writing, general notes and magic spells; anything that appeals to you or calls upon you in the moment.

Intuitive writing is one of the most natural ways to tune into the energy of your surroundings and an opportunity to release something ready and ripe from your unconscious, which through writing becomes conscious. It is as if you are digging in the Earth and suddenly you come across a small shoot of a plant, which needs water to grow. That's the moment you sit down and "pour" your expressive juice upon that seed seeking light and when it is finished very often there is a flow, clarity and a purpose to the piece you have created. Whatever you write about is never lost; it is stored in the container of that expression in the moment, which rests within the universal consciousness. Someone somewhere will need and find it one day and if nothing else you will have spent a few minutes beautifully answering your soul's call through writing.

Exercises

- Every morning, record a few things that come to you intuitively. No editing or judgement. I love this exercise and you will find there will be insights you don't expect.
- Try letter writing to aspects of yourself, e.g. to a mother

within you, to a child within you corresponding to the Triple Goddess aspects.
- Write a rhyming spell of your own listening to your intuition.

Conclusion

Full Moon Ritual

I would like to conclude this book with a Full Moon Ritual. It ties energies together in a culmination of all we have discussed and links in perfectly with stepping into our sacred, divine, feminine power and remaining there with complete trust, awareness and unconditional love. Standing in the Full Moon light, stretch your hands in front of you, palms up, so that the light shines upon them. Then say:

I call upon Thee, Lady of the Moon! Let me share this time with Thee, and let Thy Divine essence flow into me.

As you absorb the powerful moon light through your palms allow the light to spread through your body until the whole of you glows. Spend as much time with the energy as you need to.

With Love and Honour So Mote It Be!

Intuitive Witch's tip

The greater the need, the better spells work and intuitively you will know when your need is the greatest. I don't perform spells regularly and often wait for an intuitive message and remain open to it before creating and casting a spell. Details of a spell will also come intuitively along with the day/time/approach. I suggest you don't cast a spell if unsure, instead wait.

* * *

I hope you found the information in this book useful, empowering and inspiring and enjoyed the journey of discovering your own intuitive ways of working with magic, casting spells and applying it to your spiritual practice overall.

I wish you much love and many blessings on your beautiful and unique journey!

Bibliography and Further Reading

Arroyo, S. (1975) *Astrology, Psychology and the Four Elements; An energy approach to Astrology & Its Use in the Counselling Arts*, A CRCS Publication

Blackie, S. (2016) *If Women Rose Rooted: The Power of the Celtic Woman*, September Publishing

Chodorow, J. (1997) *Jung on Active Imagination*, Princeton Paperbacks

Cortright, B. (1997) *Psychotherapy and Spirit*, State University of New York Press

Cunningham, S. (2013) *Earth Power, technique of natural magic*, Llewellyn Publications

Cunningham, S. (2007) *Wicca, A guide for the solitary practitioner*, Llewellyn Worldwide

D'Este, S. (2008) *Towards the Wiccan Circle; a practical introduction to the principles of Wicca*, Avalonia

Green, M. (2002) *A Witch Alone, Thirteen Moons to Master Natural Magic*, Thorsons

Jennings, P. (2002) *Pagan Paths*, Rider Books

Johnson, R. A. *Inner Work, Using dreams and Active Imagination for Personal Growth*, HarperCollins e-books

Plotkin, B. (2003) *Soulcraft: Crossing into the Mysteries of Nature and Psyche*, New World Library, Novato, California

Sabin, T. (2013) *Wicca for beginners, fundamental of Philosophy & Practice*, Llewellyn Worldwide

Siddons Heginworth, I. (2008) *Environmental Arts Therapy and the Tree of Life*, Spirit's Rest

Starhawk, (2005) *The Earth Path*, Harper Collins Publishers

Wilber, K. (2001) *No Boundary, Eastern and Western Approaches to Personal Growth*, Shambhala

Van der Hoeven, J. (2013) *Dancing with Nemetona*, Moon Books

Van der Hoeven, J. (2012) *Zen Druidry: Living a Natural Life, with Full Awareness*, Moon Books

About the Author

Natalia Clarke is a transpersonal psychotherapist, writer, nature lover and an intuitive practitioner. Her interests lie in the human psyche, transformation, nature-based spirituality, spiritual self-awareness, earth-based spiritual practice, Scotland and UK travel. She is a poet, fiction and non-fiction writer with a passion for nature, Scotland, emotions and magic. She writes about intuitive living, magical practice, nature spirituality and soul relationship with the land.

**MOON
BOOKS**

PAGANISM & SHAMANISM

What is Paganism? A religion, a spirituality, an alternative belief system, nature worship? You can find support for all these definitions (and many more) in dictionaries, encyclopaedias, and text books of religion, but subscribe to any one and the truth will evade you. Above all Paganism is a creative pursuit, an encounter with reality, an exploration of meaning and an expression of the soul. Druids, Heathens, Wiccans and others, all contribute their insights and literary riches to the Pagan tradition. Moon Books invites you to begin or to deepen your own encounter, right here, right now. If you have enjoyed this book, why not tell other readers by posting a review on your preferred book site.
Recent bestsellers from Moon Books are:

Journey to the Dark Goddess
How to Return to Your Soul
Jane Meredith
Discover the powerful secrets of the Dark Goddess and transform your depression, grief and pain into healing and integration.
Paperback: 978-1-84694-677-6 ebook: 978-1-78099-223-5

Naming the Goddess
Trevor Greenfield
Naming the Goddess is written by over eighty adherents and scholars of Goddess and Goddess Spirituality.
Paperback: 978-1-78279-476-9 ebook: 978-1-78279-475-2

Shamanic Reiki
Expanded Ways of Working with Universal Life Force Energy
Llyn Roberts, Robert Levy
Shamanism and Reiki are each powerful ways of healing; together,
their power multiplies. *Shamanic Reiki* introduces techniques to
help healers and Reiki practitioners tap ancient healing wisdom.
Paperback: 978-1-84694-037-8 ebook: 978-1-84694-650-9

Pagan Portals – The Awen Alone
Walking the Path of the Solitary Druid
Joanna van der Hoeven
An introductory guide for the solitary Druid, *The Awen Alone* will
accompany you as you explore, and seek out your own place
within the natural world.
Paperback: 978-1-78279-547-6 ebook: 978-1-78279-546-9

A Kitchen Witch's World of Magical Herbs & Plants
Rachel Patterson
A journey into the magical world of herbs and plants, filled with
magical uses, folklore, history and practical magic. By popular
writer, blogger and kitchen witch, Tansy Firedragon.
Paperback: 978-1-78279-621-3 ebook: 978-1-78279-620-6

Medicine for the Soul
The Complete Book of Shamanic Healing
Ross Heaven
All you will ever need to know about shamanic healing and how to
become your own shaman…
Paperback: 978-1-78099-419-2 ebook: 978-1-78099-420-8